F.U.C.K the Naysayers

A Queen Making King Moves

ATIYA JOHNSON

Cover Art by Christian Cuan
Cover Photograph by Dan Sorrell
Printed in the United States of America.
First Printing, June 2021
ISBN 978-0-5789235-9-8
Legacy Learning Books
PO Box 1777 Bellmawr, NJ 08099
www.legacylearningbooks.com

I dedicate this book to my Mother-in-Law Pamela Johnson. The woman who came in and saw the potential in me at 2 years old. The woman who said "Who's baby is this? She's going to marry my son. You are an amazing mother-in-law who built a marvelous husband for me.
The love you gave and continue to give your son is unconditional.

You are an amazing mom to him, an incredible grandmother to your grands and an exceptional Mother-in-Law to me. Thank you for continuing to pour into Dwayne because he continues to pour into me. Thank you for seeing the beauty, intelligence, and commitment in me before I knew what any of those words meant as a baby. Dwayne is who he is because of you and I can't thank you enough for that. I love you Ole Lady.

To my beautiful children: Dayanna, Anisah, DJ--I pray one day this book becomes a blueprint for you to tell your naysayers "Watch me work"! Mommy loves you all!

Dayanna   *Anisah*   *Dwayne aka DJ*

Acknowledgements

There are so many people in my life who deserve and have my appreciation for their aid in making this book possible. To my husband who told me be bold, tell your story, and create a title that will help the masses. I thank you for being my rock. When times are tough for me you try to carry the weight and take it off me. You are my connection, my support, my protector, my provider. You offered not only emotional support, but insightful substantive commentary as well. Many nights saying "babe you gotta get this book out stop playing." Without your push there probably wouldn't be a book. Thank you, babe!

To my Mother the person who gave me life. I want to start off by saying I truly love and appreciate everything you do for me. Your love, loyalty, and dedication are unmatched. You taught me how to love the beauty industry. You've told me many stories to help shape who I am today and the way I see this industry. You are such a strong, loving, caring yet Fierce, Unapologetic, Committed, Kueen.

To my Dad thank you for teaching me how to always stand up and speak up for myself. Thank you for teaching me that giving up is never an option. Thank you for naming me Atiya (A beautiful gift from God) the very name that gave me the courage to be a blessing to others. You have given me the fight I needed to get through this journey of my life. You protected us as we were growing up and continue to protect us as adults. You always give the best advice. You keep us laughing and continue to instill the importance of love and discipline into our daily lives. I heard you say many times "I'm writing my book" which gave me the courage to write one myself. You have helped me become who I am through all the love and faith you have provided and all the amazing lessons you have taught. Without you and mom this book wouldn't be possible. Thank you for teaching me that helping others is what's most important in life. I thank God for blessing me with amazing parents I love and thank you!

To my one and only *bestest* sister Ayanna, I love you with all my heart. You have been instrumental in this journey with reminding me of the strength and power our parents instilled in us. In times of victory, you're my greatest cheerleader. In times of struggle, you're my second protector next to Dwayne. You are a force that pushes me and reminds everyone else of the strength of our sisterly bond. The epitome of "when they see Me, they see You".

To my two best friends Latisee and Devon, you two ladies had my back at times I couldn't think or speak. Tise, you are the very definition of a rider. Throughout this journey, you continued to stay loyal. I never had to question your love and dedication for the mission. I told you I was doing a spiritual fast and you asked, "okay, when are we starting" (almost passing out doing so ha-ha). Thank you for being my triple best friend and an undeniable support to me in my time of need.

To my other triple best friend, Devon, I would be remiss if I did not recognize all the skill and efficiency of you. You helped me improve many things in the book and in my life. You gave me encouraging words day after day, night after night. You protected my peace and my mind. Thank you for your insightful direction and your potent efforts on the book's behalf. Thank you for backing Dwayne in bullying me to keep the title of the book lol. You are an incredible best friend, thank you for believing in me even at times when I would get on your nerves. Thank you for believing in the mission and vision.

Last but certainly not least to my publisher Namibia El and Legacy Learning Books. It is to your editorial credit that the finished product is very much improved. Thank you for staying on top of me when I missed our meetings. You have helped create a piece of work I am very proud of. A piece of work I am sure will help every individual who reads it in some way. We are not done. This is the start of a long-time book relationship. Thank you!

Foreword

It's a known fact that most Creatives are Geniuses; because of our high level of imagination and intellect many beauty and grooming professionals suffer from anxiety, self-doubt, depression, procrastination, etc. This can be discouraging challenges to overcome, especially when you're facing them alone, with little to no support accompanied by naysayers. If you can identify with any of the aforementioned characteristics, then You Are In The Right Place!!! In this book, "F.U.C.K The , (A Kueen Making King Moves)," Atiya Johnson explains and navigates you along her personal and professional journey as a Licensed Master Cosmetologist, Entrepreneur, Educator, Motivational Speaker, Wife, Mother, and Woman.

She shares her compelling story on how and why she was thrust into a leadership position with the sudden "passing of the torch," from her Queen Mother, Wanda Dickerson. She highlights past and present trials, tribulations, and monumental victories. At the same time challenging and encouraging the reader to begin asking questions, growing, learning more, and thinking about your career, industry longevity, and generational wealth.

Yes, this book is for non-beauty and grooming professionals too! The book even provides a section for annotating journey entries "to fuel your fire," supercharging your engine for your marathon takeoff!!! Atiya candidly testifies how devote dedication and faith will sustain your spirit when your overcast is a down-pouring of frustration causing one to feel tremendous pain. Nonetheless through perseverance, a strategic outline and plan, mentorship, passion, and willingness to work hard...Nothing is Impossible; I'M-Possible!!

I've known Atiya and her family for multiple years. Her Queen Mother was my first Hair Care Specialist (dating back to preteen years), as well as Influencer whom inspired me to pursue my career endeavors in the cosmetology industry, once I decided to resign from the medical field. After obtaining my cosmetology license, I began working for Atiya and alongside her on various assignments. Atiya is an incredibly gifted and talented, loyal, self-motivated individual. She'll provide you with constructive criticism where needed, yet doesn't tell you what you want to hear, rather what you need to know from her heart with love. She's truly a rare find in an industry driven by image, birthing illusions of superficial grandeur and egotistical (some, not all). Creatives thriving to be King or Queen of the coveted #1Hairstylist/Barber illustrious title, Atiya still maintains integrity and dignity with humility and grace. Her disciplined work ethics were instilled in her from onset; deriving from two self-made and successful entrepreneur parents, whom are activists, educators, and pioneers in the community and universally. Therefore, it's very befitting that at this stage in her career she chronicles *How It Started versus How It Is Now.*

    Upon completion of this book, I felt exhilarated and in that very moment did as Atiya instructed, took a leap of faith and called "the salon in my area" I've been pondering over for the past year prior to COVID and lockdown; inquiring about their hiring Instagram post. I'm currently undergoing the interview process, yet I'm hopeful that what is meant to be WILL BE and Is ALREADY DONE!!

    Atiya's endurance, spirit and electrifying personality via her words was the anecdote combo of motivational stimulant and confidence reassurance I needed to refocus my aspirations towards fulfilling the purpose driven life designed for me, ordained by God.

    When you embrace Atiya's words of wisdom, you won't be able to resist the compelling feelings overcoming your yearning for more out of life and yourself, the wit to work diligently and smarter and receiving every "No" as a lesson preparing you for your abundantly spectacular blessing(s). You'll begin to examine yourself and life decisions with great anticipation of making adequate choices to produce constructive and positive changes. So, when you're faced with inevitable obstacles moving forward, you'll be equipped with a Renewed, Educated, Optimistic and FIERCE Prosperous Mindset conquer, achieve, and win!! Stay Tuned for Atiya's upcoming moves, my intuition strongly senses a sequel in the future.

Adjoa Blankson

CEO of Adjoa Amour, LLC

Licensed Master Cosmetologist in GA & NJ

Lifestyle Editor

Realtor Practitioner

Table of Contents

Introduction

I was inspired to write this book after I realized how many millionaires the beauty industry has been responsible for creating. Oftentimes, the industry is overlooked and frowned upon by people who have no clue at all. Forgive me in advance for the simplicity. I am not trying to create the next genius piece of work through sesquipedalian conversation. My focus is to create and inspire the beauty industry's next biggest sensation. In this book, it is my hope to make you aware of where you are in life and this industry. Before I do that, it is imperative that I let you know that this book became my purpose. The problem you'll read about in later chapters became the bridge I had to cross. A question I asked myself after listening to a TD Jakes sermon, "Atiya, what were you born to fix?" I want to tell you whatever battle you're going through isn't yours it's the Lords. Sometimes you must go through a **Problem** to get to your *Promise!* I want you to ask yourself: "What was I born to fix?"

An Authors Prayer:

Dear God,

   Thank you for this beautiful day.
Thank you for giving me the chance to see this day.
Thank you for loving me despite my sins.

   Forgive me for all my sins even the ones committed unknowingly. As I start this book, I pray for your guidance and your protection. Direct my path and teach me the right things to say and write. Let my words and my actions be ones that bring honor to your Holy Name. Thank you, Lord for an answered prayer.

   Through Jesus Christ I Pray.
   Amen

I want you to be able to debunk everything you've ever heard about the beauty industry. I want you to start thinking outside the box. I want you to start thinking about everyone in your life who told you that what you are doing isn't for you. If you've ever been told to go to college, but you knew college was not the right path for you ---continue reading. If you were told you don't make any money in the beauty industry --- continue reading. If you ever felt your friends, siblings etc. are making more money than you which made them more worthy ---keep reading. If you don't know if you're in the right place in life now ---keep reading. I want you to tell your naysayers you will always be a **F**ierce, **U**napologetic, **C**ommitted, **K**ueen.

I struggled with coming up with a good title for this book because it was more than just my journey. This book means more to me than just words on pages. It is a personal piece of work which allowed me to clearly see who I was becoming as I wrote these words. My amazing husband, Dwayne, who I love tremendously, came up with the title. I said, "Babe that is too bold, too straight forward, too audacious." He asked, "Babe, are you bold or average?" At that very moment, I realized the title had to be F.U.C.K the Naysayers.

I realized that if I didn't have a bold title, I would be doing the industry a disservice because we are bodacious, we are powerful, we are bold, we are courageous, but most importantly we are fearless. This title is very bold, controversial, and unapologetic. Forgive me if I offended you with the title and rawness, but I realized for me to be an inspiration to others I had to commit to bravery! I encourage you to go through this book and find yourself within it. Identify your journey and where you are within your journey. Most importantly, remember to never give up on your journey!

Disclaimer: As you begin to read the pages in this book you will see how my journey shifts. You will hear me cuss a bit, you will feel my tears, and at times, you will even hear me speak about God. The reality is I am who I am! I am raw and uncut, but also a God fearing Young Kueen.

Chapter 1:
Get Excited!

Many people fret at the idea of saying "I'm a hairstylist". I'm sure you thought to yourself, "I'd rather not tell anyone what I do for a living." Most hair stylists will not even pass out a card. To be a success in this field you must be willing to talk and connect. We get excited to connect when we're in our element at a hair show or seminar. However, when we get in a space other than beauty professionals we tend to divert. I say this is due to "FEAR," False Evidence Appearing Real. Some may say they didn't feel it was necessary at that time. I want to dig a little deeper and understand this is solely due to what we have been brainwashed to believe. For example, in the inner city a lot of guys I went to school with were trained to believe if they get into sports, for instance football, they have a better chance of making it in life. Most inner-city children were not taught the facts. According to Reference.com the NFL Players Association calculates the chances of any high school senior making it to the NFL are about 0.2 percent. This percentage is based on the statistic that only about 215 out of every 100,000 make it. Taking this calculation into account It is my opinion that sports should only be an extracurricular activity to keep the guys active. However, it's not that way. I said this to say, what should be taught in school is the very thing most inner-city public schools shy away from. That is business and entrepreneurship. Your chances of making it as an entrepreneur is higher than an NFL all-star player. According to Forbes.com, the chances of an entrepreneur's first startup ending in success is about 20%. Yet still, those odds are much better than 0.2% making it to the NFL.

Even if you don't know how much money you've made or will make doing hair. I can tell you the potential to make a massive amount of money is greater than most industries. This statement comes from my opinion and my 18years of experience in the industry.

With these facts why are we so afraid to shout and be excited about being a hairstylist. If the only thing you heard all day and everyday was, "you should go to beauty school." Then that statement was followed up with facts on the numbers and potential, you would be very excited to go. However, the problem is most people heard the total opposite. Therefore, it makes you continue to hear the naysayers, causing your fire to burnout. They told you, to be successful, you need to go to college. They told you, play it safe get a good job, get married, have children, buy a house, buy a car, and live the American dream.

You see what they did not tell you is that having a trade is the most single thing you can do to have job security. No matter what the economy is doing, the world will still need: electricians, plumbers, builders, carpenters, painters, barbers, and it damn sure needs hair stylists!! According to statecollegeofbeauty.com: The United States Bureau of Labor Statistics predicts employment opportunities for barbers, hairstylists and cosmetologists will grow by 13 percent between 2016 and 2026, which is faster than average across occupations.

I grew up in a house with a mom who was a licensed beautician in Pennsylvania and New Jersey. She has over 45 years of experience in the beauty industry. Both of my parents were entrepreneurs. My father was the proud owner of a television repair shop. *Any TV, VCR, computer* or other electronics, my father could fix it.

Mom and Dad

He was known in the town as *TV Bob.* My parents then went on to open a community center and karate school in Camden, New Jersey. My siblings all went to college, I decided to follow the footsteps of my parents. I was the child who appeared to be less of a success because I didn't go to college. My dad drilled in my head and my siblings head, "Atiya is going to be loaded with money, y'all will be begging her to borrow money!" However, I don't know if he actually believed it himself. It's possible he wanted to use the reverse psychology method to push me harder. Either way he fueled my fire to push even harder to become a success, to become an innovator, to become the youngest black woman to own her own salon and beauty school in New Jersey!

I had to decide how big I wanted to become and how big I wanted my business to become. I want the world to know me for being the biggest cosmetology enthusiast to ever do it! Yes, I love what I do! I will shout it to the world, "Yes, I am a hairstylist! Ask yourself, "am I this excited?" Be honest or you will only cheat yourself.

A hairstylist by definition is **a person who cuts and styles people's hair professionally.** You see this definition is diminishing within itself. If you ask me, I would say, a hairstylist is a person who most people confide in, a person who supports, encourages, and is constantly building others' self-esteem. A hairstylist is a creative genius, one who must know anatomy, physiology, geometrical shapes, facial shapes, current events, not to mention keeping up on the latest and greatest styles.

When the shutdown of COVID 19 happened, we were one of the most missed industries. Viral memes popped up all over the internet. Memes showing the millions of people who would bombard salon doors once the governor allowed us to open. According to Forbes.com, the beauty industry is a $532-billion-dollar global industry that will continue to grow. However, it seems other industries understand that but the actual hairstylists do not.

Search engines will tell you varied numbers on this. I believe the potential for almost every individual in the beauty industry to be a million-dollar empire is strong. However, it takes lots of action to become that sought after individual, but you must put in the work. I understand this and because of it I am enthused to holler those words, I won't stop until I get the world to believe that being a hairstylist or having a trade is the best decision you could ever make. If you're a person who loves serving and hone in on your creative side be proud to say "I'M A HAIRSTYLIST."

I stopped compromising and being mediocre. I started fighting for the number one spot in my business. I had to make a choice that no matter what others thought of the cosmetology industry I was going to be EXCITED about every inch of the industry. I told myself, "Atiya, your energy has to be contagious."

When I started listening to Grant Cardone, I would hear him say you must be obsessed, or you'll be average. This is what it means to be obsessed versus average.

OBSESSED HAIR STYLIST	MEDIOCRE (AVERAGE) HAIR STYLIST
Always looking to serve the client.	Does not go above and beyond.
Stays overtime	Leaves early and works less days.
Always has a great attitude.	Has a negative attitude that shows outwardly?
Sees the endless possibility in all things.	Always thinking negative.
The hardest worker in the salon.	Pricing exceeds their value.
Does everything to ensure client satisfaction.	Does not know what success looks like for them.
Understands success is their duty. Does more than what is asked of them.	Underworks never over delivers.
Constantly learning.	Stops learning.
Has an open mind.	Does not like change.

The moment my ideology changed about who I am, was the moment my dad said, "you're just twirling curls". Yes, he diminished my craft, and the industry I was excited to have as my livelihood to just "a twirl of a curl." I remember it like it was yesterday. It was a pivotal moment when I asked myself "what's wrong with being a hairstylist?" That day my dad called a staff meeting for our community center.

I was born and raised in Camden, New Jersey, once known as the most dangerous city in America. My parents developed a community center in the heart of the city in a little store front building. There they raised hundreds of successful individuals. My father is the definition of success, yet he couldn't see my success.

I love my father unconditionally, which is why he was the one person with the ability to make me realize my potential with just four words, "you're just twirling curls." At any rate, my dad called this meeting for all lead members of his community center. On that call, he went around introducing everyone, well actually he introduced how we should introduce ourselves. He said, Jamal (my oldest brother) you can say "I'm Jamal Dickerson a music teacher of 20 years, I am the Milken award winning Teacher of the year etc. Understand these accomplishments that my brother has are tremendous. They are not accomplishments to be taken lightly. Milken Teacher of the year is a national honor not something only New Jersey recognizes. Teacher Magazine nicknamed the program the "Oscars of Teaching."

My dad went on to introduce my other brother, Nasir, then one of the other leadership members. He went on and on announcing and introducing members of our center. He finally got to me and said these words verbatim "yeah, Atiya you can say something like, I twirl curls." One of the members then came off mute to laugh hard, that person was my nephew. My little nephew, the one who's diaper I once changed, the one I give money to all the time. Can you imagine how small this made me feel?

I don't want you to read this and think I'm for one second saying my siblings aren't accomplished. All we want as humans is for the people who mean the most to you to see you. So many emotions ran through me in that very moment. I went from being embarrassed to being angry. I wanted to yell to every person on that call. Thinking back my mind ran wild. I thought to myself, you need to stand up for yourself. I was always taught to speak my mind as a child. *"With all due respect, I need everyone on this call to eat my Ass."* Coming back to reality my response was nothing at all. See somethings are left better unsaid. It's no need to be mean, become Successful!

When I tell you the two little people, we're playing a game of tug a war with my mind. I wanted to shout, "Dad F you" and everyone else who believes and agrees with what they just heard. Of course, I couldn't say that ha-ha, my dad is not one to play with or disrespect. I was infuriated because I knew there was nothing I could do or say that was going to make me feel better. What I felt didn't matter in that moment, the remedy to proving someone wrong is doing the work. Becoming so successful they start to look at their failures, instead of worrying about you!

For anyone reading this book, I know you have that one person you want to see your accomplishments and your potential. You may think they never truly see you. Trust me when I tell you that your nay-sayers see you. The problem is not you, don't take it personal. The truth is there is something within that person of unhappiness. Misery loves company, while trying to accomplish their goal but not being successful may cause a bit of jealousy with anyone else doing so. They can't understand you because they are not you. Yes, maybe that sounds very cliche and small, but you can't expect anyone to understand your accomplishments if they're still battling theirs.

Don't look for people to praise you and see you. Start with seeing and believing in you, and fight like hell to become so successful they will always remember your name.

Disclaimer: *My Dad is many things to me; a naysayer isn't something I wanted him to be but in that moment, he was "the naysayer." He has always supported me as an independent entrepreneur because that's who he is and that's what he believes in. However, he didn't believe the beauty industry was anything more than twirling a curl, like many others. Just remember, you must be able to identify certain things said and done from YOUR naysayer.*

I got off that call feeling mortified for many reasons. I felt like I should have expressed myself. I felt like I missed the opportunity to speak up for the industry, but I didn't know what to do to change the narrative.

I hung up the phone and started discussing it with my husband. He knew I was hurting and wanted my hurt to stop, but I don't think he understood the depth of my pain. He told me, "Babe, it's OK. Use that comment to fuel your fire!" He said, "If your own family don't realize how much of a success you are...how can you expect anyone too?"

At that very moment, I told myself that's it. I asked myself what's wrong with being who I am? What's wrong with me deciding college wasn't the path for me? What's wrong with feeling good about "twirling a curl?" What's wrong with being a great hairstylist? You see what my husband made me realize was, for others to be excited about who I am, I had to first be excited and realize there is absolutely nothing wrong with twirling a curl. There is nothing wrong with being a hairstylist!!!

My dad doesn't realize how he motivated me to become something I never envisioned with four simple words..."you're just twirling curls". Dad, if you're reading this I thank you for being the push I needed. I thank you for being the one person I needed to push me beyond my limits. I thank you for being thee, Robert Dickerson!

In the next chapters, you'll read why it's imperative that you realize who you are and why you are who you are to tap into your potential. You will read that there is absolutely, without a shadow of a doubt, endless potential in being a hairstylist. If you are someone reading this book and you are not a hairstylist, I encourage you to continue reading. Inevitably you will be able to see yourself in the chapters of this book. If you are thinking I went to college, I just picked this book up because of the title, you should keep reading.

Lesson 1

Think about the naysayers in your life, some you probably didn't realize were naysayers. Use these lines to write down 3 people who killed your dream, but you will now use them to fuel your fire and push harder.

1. _____

2. _____

3. _____

Think about a time you felt under-supported by someone who mattered most to you. What have/will you do to use that person to push you closer to success?

_____

_____

Think and write down three people you will surround yourself with moving forward. These three people should be people who will encourage and help push you past your limits.

1. _____

2. _____

3. _____

Chapter 2:
What's Wrong With Being A Hairstylist?

As I thought about the title of this chapter, I thought, "What's wrong with being a hairstylist?" This chapter will probably be the most important chapter of this entire book. Here you will find the reason why I decided to write this book. Many people think it's taboo to be a hairstylist. They tell themselves I don't want anyone to know that I'm a hairstylist. Being a hairstylist doesn't have any notoriety to it. They believe because of what they were told, success is not made for hairstylists. They believe I didn't go to college because I wasn't smart enough.

Another thing I've heard is I didn't have enough money to go to college, so I picked up the trade. Many people think hairstylists don't make money (I think that's the most ridiculous thought process a person can have).

If you want to talk about an industry where money is unlimited, this is the industry. Not only is the money endless, but the potential is endless! The beauty industry potential is endless although many people think it stops at "twirling a curl". You can become a Cosmetologist (which by the way is much different than a beautician), aesthetician, a nail technician, a barber, a beautician, a product creator, a celebrity stylist ---the list goes on and on and on.

All the above titles are beauty industry-based activities that only begin to scratch the surface. If you're currently in the beauty industry and think this field is not a tremendous accomplishment, you need to reevaluate your "Why."

You need to start thinking about why you entered this industry to begin with. Many people have reached stardom being in the beauty industry, while others understand they need to get in the beauty business even if they never imagined they would be.

Take for instance Kim Kimble, a widely known celebrity hairstylist who does Beyoncé's hair, among many others. She became famous because Beyoncé put a video out and everybody wanted to know who did those long 50 to 60-inch lemonade braids on her hair. Few people knew who she was before learning of her being Beyoncé stylist. She created a masterpiece on Beyoncé's hair and continues to create magic on many other celebs. Several of her styles became staple styles. They become iconic styles, which causes those styles to be sought after.

If I interviewed Kim Kimball today, I'm almost certain she would say the same thing many hairstylists have said at one time or another. That is. "I didn't initially think being a hairstylist would take to the heights. I've conquered today. I didn't think initially that being a hairstylist was worthy of the energy that I'm putting into it. I didn't think being a hairstylist was something to say I was proud of. I didn't think being a hairstylist was the definition of success. The moment Beyoncé walked into her doors I'm sure Kim Kimble's entire mindset shifted. I would even bet hers shifted way before that point in her career (if it had not shifted, she would have never made it to that point).

I don't know if Kim Kimball's parents were like my parents. I don't know if her parents were like your parents. Maybe your parents, friends, spouse, and/ or your relatives told you that being a hairstylist is not anything of notoriety. Maybe they told you you'll have tons of money (like my dad told me), yet they don't believe it themselves. Maybe they told you being a hairstylist is an amazing thing, and if they did, I love them for telling you that. The point is whether good or bad, everyone has an opinion.

Taking or listening to their opinion is up to you to decide. I have built a confidence so strong that I could care less what others think about what I'm doing. My only purpose is to help others be better versions of themselves and get filthy rich doing so. If that means using the beauty industry as my main vehicle, what others think doesn't concern me. I bleed the beauty industry---I love it, I'm excited to say I'm a hairstylist and I encourage you to start doing the same.

You see when you live to help others in whatever way you are doing so, your life becomes very rewarding. For me, it is an honor to take a person from being in a vulnerable state through beauty. This industry does not discriminate! Everyone needs a stylist, barber, or nail tech. Whether it is men, women, children, or elderly, we all want to look good and feel great! I

don't care who that naysayer is; it's time for you to say...
"F.U.C.K. the naysayers!"

Understand, to achieve massive success, you must be willing to put in the work. Everything worth having takes hard work and dedication. However, many people in this field look for the easy way out. They start thinking I don't like standing for long hours, I'll become a nurse. Sorry to tell you but being a nurse is also hard work. Not to mention you no longer must worry about just standing you now have to move while standing. Many say I no longer want to do hair. I want to sit behind a desk. Sorry babes but that also involves work, and you'll probably also hate your job and boss.

The point I'm making here is the beauty industry is a very rewarding industry, however if it isn't working out for you I can almost guarantee it's you and not the industry.

I have a girlfriend who knows the potential of this industry. She has created many things including her own hair care growth line. She's been in this industry for 15 years. She understands the quality that a hairstylist possesses. She understands the amount of money you can make as a hairstylist is endless. In her heart, she knows and understands that the job that she used to have doesn't even equal up to her business that she has now. Yes, at times having a business can get very foggy. You go through ups and down. You make money and sometimes you lose money, but it is truly worth it to bet on yourself every time.

I want us to be very clear on the difference between a job, a career, and a business. Oxford languages defines a job *as a paid position of regular hours.*

It defines a career as *an occupation undertaken for a significant period of a person's life and with opportunities for progress.*

Oxford languages defines a business as *a person's regular occupation, profession, or trade.*

There's a clear difference in all three: a job simply says you're trading hours for dollars. A career starts to move in a direction of more money for more advancement. A business is not defined by the number in which one makes. Why? It is because a business cannot be defined by a number because there is no cap on the number of dollars one can make. Although you may work in someone else's salon in the beauty industry, you are still your own business. It is still your job to do whatever it takes to succeed and advance beyond your potential.

I want you to be obsessed with this industry, don't be average. Leave average to industries outside of us. You see beauty professionals are not nine to fivers. We can sometimes be 9am to 1am. We can sometimes be 9am to 12pm. We can sometimes be 24/7, or we can even be 365 days a year! It all depends on the amount of action you want to take and how far you want your life and career to go.

My girlfriend left a well-paid 9-to-5 job to become a hairstylist. She now has a career that she loves. She wakes up every morning excited about going to her business. She understands she is no longer a slave to a 9-to-5 job. She's an owner, a boss lady of a business that she can continuously put all her energy into and excel. However, my girlfriend makes it her point to let everyone know she used to be an engineer. I agree with her being an engineer is a major accomplishment, but then she chose to change paths to the beauty industry for a reason. She's very talented, and a beast of many techniques. Yet she still questions her talent, questions her money, and questions the industry. I once told her like my Uncle G (Grant Cardone) told me, "you don't have to be the best, you just have to be the best known".

In other words, you don't have to be the most talented person, you just must get enough attention to make tons of money! Why? It is because money follows attention. Not only does she know being in this industry has made her tons of money. She also chose to stay in it for fifteen years. I've said to her many times we know you were an engineer 15 years ago but what are you now! She mentions she was an engineer so often to the point where it got on my nerves and forced me to put the scenario in this book.

Oftentimes we as a people try to validate our prior successes instead creating new success daily. Understanding what this industry is all about and what it has to offer is not an issue she has. Her issue is validation. Society told her the beauty industry is not valid enough. Her naysayers, whoever they were or may still be, will have her believe being an engineer is much better than being a hairstylist. She knows and has proven facts that show contrary.

When most people think of success coming from a certain industry, the hair industry doesn't normally make that equation. The hair industry is looked at as one of those things of "oh that's cute". I'm sure your parents, family members, boyfriend, girlfriend or maybe even you, think it's nothing worth real value. I'm here to tell you it's worth value beyond measure. It is worth shouting to the top of the mountains, "I am a hairstylist!!!". The moment you start to gain real success and notoriety you'll start to shout it louder and louder.

I can't think of one individual on planet earth who at some point in time must groom their hair. Even if they took a kitchen knife and cut all the growing hair off, that is still doing something with your hair. A homeless person living on the streets, at some point will go into a barbershop or do it himself for whatever the occasion may be. See folks who aren't doing it will never understand what it takes to be a hairstylist. Your naysayer most times never worked a day in the industry. They can't understand the gratitude we get by watching one's persona and self-esteem rise as they look at themselves in the mirror. I live to make sure I do what I do for a greater cause.

I was blessed to be part of this business at a young age, and I am so thankful I was. If you're young like I was and you know the only thing you can think about when you wake up in the morning is whose hair am I doing today, this field is for you. Don't let your parents sell you into an American dream of bad debt by going to college. Do I want you to hate college? Absolutely not! Am I trying to sell you on the beauty industry? YES! I most definitely am! I know what the industry has to offer.

I've experienced some of the endless potential and yet I'm still just scratching the surface. I want you to understand that in America there are five classifications of wealth. Ranging from top to bottom: 1) Wealthy, 2) upper middle class, 3) middle class, 4) lower middle class, and 5) poverty. Many of your naysayers are living between poverty and middle class. Those two classifications are suffering badly. Which makes me begin to encourage you to ask: "Should I honestly listen to people living at levels I'm trying to exceed?"

The reality is people in the top two tiers of the pyramid are willing to teach you how to do what you love while making bank from it. I don't want you to get in this industry or stay in this industry without striving to make bank. I want you to have clarity. I want you to be very specific. For you to change your naysayer's mind, you must have CERTAINTY. If you're not certain about what you want to do and how you want to do it, you can't make someone else be certain in your decision. You should be so specific that it leaves your parents speechless when you tell them I refuse to follow your path of poverty. Most of my colleagues in the industry are financially supporting their parents and relatives because they were certain about being a Cosmetologist.

My best friend knew what she wanted to do while we were in high school. She knew she wanted to pursue a career to be an orthopedic surgeon. This would have taken her 14 years minimum to even finish the education. According to ZipRecruiter.com she would've been making 350-400k per year. She of course also would have been in bad debt of about 200,000 or more. Understand, this career has a cap on it. My best friend would've been making enough money to put her between the middle class and upper middle-class range of America. However, she would have always had a cap on what else she could do in her field. It's not a business that is scalable, unlike the beauty industry where there are many different options (career paths) in that same industry.

My bestie would have eventually had to start doing something else outside of her field to bring in additional income. One day in high school she came up to me and asked; "best friend what are you going to do after we graduate"? I said, "go work in my mom's salon". Before I go on, I want you to understand the family dynamic we came from. She grew up in a single mother household. Her mom was a very good school principal in Pennsylvania. So of course, most of the time in her house she heard talks about going to college.

I grew up in a two-parent household of which my parents allowed us to make educated decisions on our own. My parents both had a business. However, all my siblings went to college and are currently working in the educational field. I was the only child to choose a different path and followed the footsteps of my Mother (who was pregnant with me while in beauty school). I don't say all this to discredit my friend. I say this to give you a different perspective so you can come to a sound decision if you're stuck in the middle of one.

I told my girlfriend I'm going to work in my mom's salon. She then asked me "bestie why don't you want to go to college?" I replied, "I'm more interested in making money straight out of high school. I don't want to wait 4 or 14 years to start making the money."

Here's the sad reality if my bestie would've taken the path of an orthopedic surgeon. By the time she graduated school; I would have surpassed her income probably about three times over. The problem with us hairstylists is money management. We earn the money quickly and it leaves us more quickly (which by the way is a problem for most Americans, not just hairstylists). My Dad always said, "the more money you make the more money you spend."

There were two reasons my girlfriend asked me that question (even though we were in a trade school). Hear me on this, we both graduated from Camden County Technical School in New Jersey. She graduated in the field of allied health. I graduated in the field of cosmetology. This school was meant for people who knew they wanted to be in a trade-based business or industry.

She asked me the question for two reasons. I was always a smart cookie. I graduated in the top 8% of my class and was able to attend college for the first two years free of charge. The first reason is that she wanted me to take advantage of the opportunity that was presented in front of me. The second reason is because all her life, the only option she knew or was trained to know was GO TO COLLEGE.

My friend wanted the best for me and what the best for me meant to her was go to college and obtain a degree. Even though you have no clue what would interest you enough to stay in school for a minimum of four more years. A lot of people take 4 years to do a 2- year college course. Was my friend a naysayer? No, she was just someone who believed at that time the only way to success is college. I guarantee if you ask her today you will find her thought process totally changed. You see I was certain. I had a very clear vision, and although that vision shifted more times than not. One thing remained, I graduated with a license in cosmetology, and I was going to make it happen. I showed her, and I'm still showing her you can succeed without going to college. There are many ways to skin a cat. You must find which works best for you and commit to nothing but success.

I have a client who is going through a state of depression. She actually uses depression medicine to be able to cope with life daily. One of the things that gives her satisfaction and makes her feel better is when she's in the salon. When she comes into my salon and I do her hair and make her feel like the world still loves her, that is her satisfaction. She was one who went to college and sacrificed her love life among other things for her career. She tells me all the time how she regrets that choice. I can't say how she feels her life was altered because we never got into details. If I had to guess, I would say she probably would have continued her relationship with her fiancé at that time instead of choosing to go to college longer. I believe the dots in life are meant to connect and everything is ordained through God. So maybe her choosing that path was right but it also could've been wrong if the choices were made based on what society says is right. We heard our parents and society tell us things like: *Money doesn't grow on trees. A penny earned is a penny saved. College equals success. Don't talk to strangers etc.* Most of these ideologies are very contradictory, but if you hear them long enough you believe them. Instead, we should be thinking *my network equals my net-worth.* Which means I should talk to strangers to build my list of contacts.

Like my bestie, she was trained to believe the only way to success was college. That very idea is what is causing my client to live a life of depression today. Although she has used every dating site there is, she has still been stagnant in her dating life. Here's the problem for my client, because her mind is so clouded on whether she made the right decision or not with putting college before love, she can't make a sound decision within any other relationship. I don't think she understands what is happening. When you're uncertain at one point or another in your life, you allow others to dictate your path. She even mentioned to me how she had the man of her dreams while she was in college. He wanted to have children and marry her, but she wasn't interested in that plan. Pursuing her career and getting her degree was a better plan for her.

Look at the wealth pyramid below.

Wealthy

Upper Middle Class

Lower Middle Class

Middle Class

Poverty

Wealth Pyramid

There are some common denominators within the people in the top two tiers. If you talk to the majority of the wealthy, they'll tell you they either dropped out of college or never attended. I'm not telling you to drop out of college or not go at all. What I am saying is sometimes you must model, mimic, and master what has already been done, instead of allowing society to dictate your path.

Look at this list of wealthy who either dropped out of college or did not go at all.

1) Bill Gates (dropped out)

2) Mark Zuckerberg (dropped out)

3) Ralph Lauren (dropped out)

4) Oprah Winfrey (never attended)

5) Beyonce (never attended)

6) Jay-Z (never attended)

Understand finances and relationships work together which is why I'm telling you this story. When one thought process far exceeds the other you can't come to common grounds with the other. Let's face it, the number one reason most relationships fail is because of finances (money). Choosing to take years of your life to pursue a career of uncertainty is the very foundation of failure. I would tell you to bet on a sure thing and that my friend is YOU! Bet on yourself and your industry and stop letting others dictate your career choices, because of what they deem to be success. I know you're probably thinking why couldn't she do both? Why did she have to choose between her love life or career? I would say to you she didn't have to choose but she did have to find another guy who was willing to wait while she continued to pursue her career. If she would've found someone who was willing to wait, they probably would've still run into problems down the road.

This isn't my relationship book, so I will leave that conversation here. However, it is a point that needs to be made to get you (the reader) to see clearly. She didn't know at that moment the decision she was about to make was going to alter her life forever. No, I'm not minimizing her career accomplishments. I just want you to think before you make a decision that may alter your life forever based on what other people think. You may be asking why can't I choose to have it all? I agree that you should have it all but the problem in this scenario was her life was altered because of what society told her was success. This ultimately caused her to never have children or find true love.

Lesson 2

1. Did you allow your naysayers words or opinion to have an impact on the choices you made in life and career?

---

2. Circle which one you are currently in:

   A. Job

   B. Career

   C. Business

3. Are you excited about your choice? Write down, what you are doing to maximize your potential.

---

4. Think about a time you felt under-supported by someone who mattered most to you. What have/will you do to use that person to push you closer to success?

Lesson 2 (continued)

5. Think about and write down three people you will
surround yourself with moving forward. These three
people should be people who will encourage and help
push you past your limits.

     1. _____

     2. _____

     3. _____

Chapter 3:
College or Beauty

As I write this, the country is going through a major economic crisis. A deadly sickness has caused us to walk the world in unheard of ways. Never in a million years did I think we would have to go to work wearing a mask. We must walk into stores with a mask on, walk in only one direction in aisles and stay 6 feet away from the person in front of us. This pandemic has caused some major issues for all parties involved. People who went to college to succeed in creating the American dream for themselves, no longer see that as the same attainable goal.

Businesses are shutting down all over this country. Fortune 500 companies are telling their employees they will no longer come into the office. New York is a major ghost town. The city we once knew as "the city that never sleeps," is sleeping heavy. There was no New Year Eve ball dropping celebration. Well actually there was a ball dropping ceremony with not one person allowed to come see it live.

We are talking about a town where people walk the streets at all times of the day. I feel like I am living in a twilight zone and I'm sure you do as well. Every store we go into is selling masks and PPE equipment. Churches are shut down, having a party with hundreds of people coming is a blast from the past. This thing is a major issue for most. Cosmetologists had to shut their business down for over three months.

One thing I want anyone reading this book to know is being in a service industry is not for everyone. You ought to be the type of person who is fine with long hours, irritated clients (at times), standing on your feet, making massive amounts of money one day, yet smaller amounts another day. When COVID-19 happened service industry businesses were shut down for months. Salons, barbershops, nail shops, spas, restaurants etc., were shut down for 3 or more consecutive months. This meant we went from making thousands of dollars a week to making zero. Some were hoping they could get to go through.

Here's the thing, while all of this was happening something else was taking place in the hearts of our clients. They started to realize how important we really were to their life. Although most people were working from home, they still had to get on video conferences. Clients quickly realized how much they needed us. While we as stylists were home struggling with making means meet. Our clients were home gaining a certain gratification and realization for us that will never disappear. People never thought about how important their hair stylist, barber, nail technician, or esthetician really was to their livelihood. While we were shut down for months not able to make one red penny doing what we love, it was a needed change.

Here is the point, moreover service industry individuals still made out better than many 9 to 5 workers. Most 9 to 5 workers went to college to get a degree, get a good paying job, and be a part of the middle class. They wanted to get a good job, nice car, house in the suburbs and live a comfortable life. These individuals during this time were laid off, fired, or quit their jobs for lack of uncertainty. I know you're wondering... *What does all this mean? What does any of this have to do with this book? Why do I have to listen to what was wrong in the world for months?* The point I am making here is, no matter where you ended up in your career or which side of the spectrum you were on; it made more sense to be in the service industry. Yes, that is a very bold claim to make, but here is why I feel it is true.

I want you to answer these next questions with transparency and honesty in your heart. To answer these questions, you must know your numbers if you're a stylist. For my college attendees/graduates,
when you went back to work after the pandemic:

- Did you receive a raise?
- When you went back to work, we're your customers at ease or easy to deal with?
- Do you have any idea if you'll be getting a Christmas bonus or any bonus?

For my industry professionals, notice I said, "industry professionals", if you are a kitchen beautician or a YouTube self-taught sensation, you may not be thinking of the things I'm about to ask. If you are a professional, you should be using some type of software like Bizlinks or Vagaro salon booking software, which will allow you to see your numbers clearly. When you returned from the pandemic:

- Were you very busy that first week?
- Were your clients/customers happy to see you? Did you make more money when you returned after the pandemic?

Why are these questions important to you? Industry professionals more than likely answered yes to all these aforementioned questions. Whereas my college attendees probably answered no to the above questions for them.

You see, when you guys went back to work the world was on edge and you ended up getting the brunt of that deal. Yet when the industry professional went back to work the environment was one that most people missed and needed. This caused clients to spend more money. It caused them to be more patient as a result of sitting at home for 3 or more months and realizing how much we were truly needed and missed.

Although the world was on edge, the beauty industry was missed. Most 9-5 workers had to deal with picking up the pieces because most of their co-workers were fired or quit. They had to deal with customers being frustrated and taking it out on them. They had to deal with getting pay cuts or no raises because companies were trying to figure out how they would stay afloat.

Industry professionals, I want you to understand the endless potential of the field you were blessed to be in. Do not take this lightly, this field is limitless. No one can tell you how much money you can make. No one can tell you that you can't get a raise. We actually gave ourselves a raise. Shops across the country implemented COVID fees, or higher prices. Clients were not reluctant to pay these additional fees because they knew the importance of having us in their lives.

You cannot have a robot to make a person look and feel good at the same time. You cannot make a robot to be one's sister, friend, counselor, therapist, or stylist. However, companies are making robots to put the everyday worker out of commission. Let's take Walmart for instance, if you went into a Walmart 10-15 years ago you saw employees all over the store. If you go into Walmart now, you see more self-serve lines. Now they have self-serve lines with the belt attached so you can become your own attendant. You also see massive, tall center tower structure for picking up your own food. The leaders of Walmart are not thinking about ways to generate more jobs. They are focusing on ways to eliminate the current jobs workers hold.

Let's think about Zoom! Zoom has become the new booming system that has eliminated the human personal connection. Watch how it will eventually eliminate your job. If I am a therapist and you're a receptionist-- why do I need you to check a client in if I can just do a Zoom call? If I have an office that I no longer utilize because I can just do Zoom calls at home--do I need the cleaning company to come clean? If I am a doctor just doing Zoom meetings to tell a client what's wrong with them-- do I need a nurse to do the preliminary work? These are just a few examples of modern-day technologies getting rid of you. If the pandemic shows you anything, I pray that it will show you why you need another plan other than college. Do not get me wrong, I am not saying anything is wrong with going to college. However, I wrote this book for my fellow industry professionals to understand that being a hairstylist is enough. Being a barber is enough. Your financial potential is endless. While you may have some ups and downs, it is a ride only you can end when you're ready. No one else can put a cap on your potential in the industry.

To understand some of the myths you may have heard, let's dive in:

Ziprecruiter.com says hairstylists make on average $14 an hour which equals out to about $29,779 a year. *When you heard that statistics did you think that's B.S.! Did you think "I change my mind; I no longer want to be a hairstylist"?* (I'll debunk this later).

According to Monster.com an associate degree holder makes about $32,700 a year with them having at least 2-4 years of experience. *When you heard this. I hope you started thinking I have about $30,000 in student loans, but for me to make close to that amount in a year I need at least 2-4 years of* *experience.* Here is the issue with this scenario, if you go to college, you have already taken out the loan. You graduate in hopes of getting a good paying job, but honestly to obtain a job that will help pay off your student loans, you need at least 2-4 years of experience. How will you get that experience? In the meantime, while you are chasing a job to pay you enough to pay your loans off, your interest rates on your loans are expanding. You now have a $30,000 loan that's quickly turning into $50,000 give or take. Don't get me wrong, I'm not downplaying college. If you were a college attendee, don't be mad at me, I'm just stating facts.

Most people who go to college come out no longer interested in the field they went to school. Many of them cannot find a job to pay them what they want for lack of experience. They turn to finding a job by any means necessary. The problem with this reality is that you went to college with all these dreams, hopes, and aspirations to deflate yourself to being average. Telling yourself "I only want to live the American dream, but the American dream begins to look more and more like a blast from the past".

Now let's debunk this $14 an hour hairstylist rate. I'll show you with real numbers why this number is so far from reality. If you work 5 days a week, doing only 2 wash and curls each day you would have made $26.66 an hour. This theory alone debunks Ziprecruiter.com. Understand this is for a person that has not attempted any advertising, did not hand out any cards, and just let their social media do absolutely nothing. To sum that up, these numbers would essentially be for a very basic mediocre stylist. Now let's get into where that math came from so you can understand why this is far from the average hairstylist.

The math: a stylist works 5 days a week, doing 2 $40 wash and curls each day. The number of hours it would take to accomplish this task on an average head) 1 ½, for a total of 3 hours a day at 5 days a week.

✂ 40 x 2= $80

✂ 80 x 5=$400

✂ <u>400 divided by 15</u>

<u>(hours of time for that week)</u> = $26.66 an hour

There is so much right with this scenario but still so much wrong. You see if you're reading this book, I want you to see the endless potential you have in being in the cosmetology industry. This math is pennies. My 15-year-old niece and daughter make more than this just practicing on friends' hair. I made way more than this at 14 years of age. Everyone in school knew I was the hairstylist without me doing any advertising. Word of mouth was my best friend. I was doing so much hair making so much money at 14 my dad got tired of people calling our house phone for me to do their hair. He immediately went out to get me a cellphone.

The point I'm making here is when Zip Recruiter came up with their math, they interviewed someone who was clearly doing wayyyyyyy less than their best. This industry is not an industry you should get into if you are not ready to make an endless amount of money. This industry is not one you should get into if you are looking to only scratch the surface as a provider. This industry is not one you should get into if being average or mediocre is an option for your life. If you want to be in an industry where most will have you believe make little money, yet we (the stylist truly making the money) know is the only career we want than keep reading. The beauty industry is a billion-dollar industry. Everyone knows the potential of the beauty industry, yet sometimes the folks who are in it cannot see it.

Allow me to show you even bigger math and numbers: Let's take a top tier technique, something that's hot right now micro-link and itip extensions. Depending on where you are in the world these numbers may look slightly different give or take. This service will range anywhere from $500 -$1,500. For the sake of easy math let's look at the average. If you charged $1,000 for the service, with the hair included, and you did this 4 times a week. You would make $4,000 a week on just this one service. That number does not include regular services throughout the rest of the week. Earning $4,000 week is on a low end with only one technique would bring in $16,000 that month. There are not many jobs paying this way at all.

This is very doable. Just do the math, then apply the action steps you need to take to make these numbers a reality. I wrote this book for all industry professionals to be excited about this industry. To know the importance and the significance of the industry they are in. It is time we stop apologizing or feeling less than because our parents told us were only twirling curls. It is time for you to push past the limits of what society says is right. It's time for you to start showing up and showing out as a hairstylist. Everywhere we go people can point out a stylist. Why is that? I'm going to get a little cocky here, it's because we have a certain air about us that stands out amongst the rest. It is because we look the part, our confidence (which most times is offensive to others in the room), our swag, the inner creativity in us that shows through so bright, the fashion forward dressing, and the fly cuts and color we exude.

The list can go on and on. All I am saying is it is time for us to be proud of who we are. **<u>Start embracing your inner ability and exuding it outwardly, so the world will see you for the beast you are.</u>** Stop caring that you did not go to college. Stop caring that people believe you don't make money. You know the truth. College is not for everyone. If you are like me, you knew being a cosmetologist was the only path you ever needed and wanted, embrace it, and live it to the fullest!

Start embracing your inner ability and exuding it outwardly so the world will see you for the beast you are!

Chapter 4:

Trials Are Stepping Stones To Greatness

At a time when all hope was lost, no money, no loans being approved, people wanting their money back. I continued to fight but it became the hardest thing in the world. Knowing my intentions were pure, the reason I wanted to become a hairstylist is because I am a people pleaser. I am a person that wants to help at all causes. I became a hairstylist because I love what I do. The biggest joy for me is seeing people love who they are by looking at themselves in the mirror.

Then all that changed, waking up in the middle of the night tears drowning my eyes. I tried to watch TV to help ease the pain, but nothing was working. The woman who once thought she would never need to talk to a therapist became the woman begging to find a therapist. I feel the frog in my throat as I write this chapter. The tears that continue to stream down my face as I try to hide the tears and the pain from my son sleeping next to me and my husband sleeping next to him. All caused by the industry I love, yet the same industry that is causing the pain as I continue to write.

My feelings of wanting to give up continues to fight the ego of knowing everyone is counting on me to make this dream come true for all of us. The pain of knowing the weight is on my shoulders because I have a team, students, children, employees, family, but most importantly a husband that loves me and supports me so much my pain becomes his pain.

Internalizing every word, I heard as I watched a tv show, reciting: *To thine own self be true...Listen to yourself and you'll find clarity.* I asked myself, "How can I find clarity? How can I be true to myself? How can I continue to fight for what I know is right?" It feels like the world is on my shoulders, but my shoulders are disintegrating. As I deal with the pain, I ask myself, is it worth fighting for? Is the industry I loved really worth fighting for? How can you really help Atiya? How can you truly change the narrative? Is it worth becoming the success you dreamed of becoming just days ago? Telling myself, it is not in your blood to give up. Giving up was never an option. Yet, thinking the people you were doing this for are fighting you the hardest. Atiya what are you going to do?

Then suddenly, the dream became real. We finally did it after two years of continuous back and forth. Text messages from Devon (my best friend and Director of Jana's Cosmetology Academy) saying "we did it!" The first black owned and operated Cosmetology Academy in New Jersey. I wake then reality slaps me in the face saying, "*it was all a dream*" (Biggie Smalls voice). Layer after layer and still no resolve. Day after day, I wake again to thoughts of it nothing more than a dream. Every day I wake up thinking today must get better, but it doesn't. While there are many small successes as I go through this process, the small successes still are not enough.

I tried to be a master rule twister. I tried to change the industry when the industry was not ready for change. I tried to show the world it is worth having a trade, yet more importantly it's worth being a cosmetologist. I tried to succeed by helping others! The question I continued to ask myself "are those same individuals still worth helping"?

As I write this chapter while being very transparent, I still have not figured that answer out. You see I am someone who has never truly had to face any real adversity. My life was great, my parents gave me everything I very rarely heard the word "NO". I met my soulmate at a very young age and continue to live an amazing life with him by my side.

Even when I thought I met adversity it turned out to be a great success. My mother suffered great lost. She lost her sister at age 15. As a fairly young adult, she lost her older brother, a year later she lost her younger brother, then a year after that she lost her mother. My mother is the true definition of a "wounded warrior". You want to talk about, if adversity was a picture of a person, it would definitely be my mother. She is a very strong woman, yet sometimes even strong has a breaking point. Losing both my uncles and grandmother was way too much at once for my mother. A nervous breakdown was inevitable for her. At that time, I was 17, coming in from school to the salon. A letter left in my drawer that read,

Atiya, I had to go, please take care of the business. We are talking about a business that had over 20 years of experience at this point. I was only 17, and all I was thinking was I want my mommy, where is she? How could she leave me? How could she leave the business like this and expect me to handle it? I am still a child. I don't know how to pay a bill? I don't know what story I'm going to tell her clients. I cannot tarnish my mom's reputation, while she's going through life's turmoil.

Think Atiya think! Go out there you have clients, your mother has clients, Tise has clients, you got to boss up. I cried and I cried because I was not sure how was I going to do this.

Reading the letter over and over and over hoping praying and wishing it was all a dream. My mother was a warrior all her life, but at this very moment I had to be the link to help hold her chain together. I went out to the front starting my mom's clients, putting conditioner on Ms. Irene. Then moving to my client getting her started only to have to move to the next client to get her started. Juggling between 3 clients at one time and avoiding the, *where's your mom conversation.* At that point, I had not figured out what the story would be to save face for my mom. I had just pulled myself up from crying my eyes out. I was not mentally prepared to have that conversation without crying.

At 17, I was forced to take on a business with over 20 years of history and make it work without tarnishing my mom's legacy. Was this adversity? Absolutely. but it was also setting me up for success. It was like throwing a baby in a pool to see what they will do. Most times they will start to swim because they are used to being in water for 9 months. It was second nature to them. Doing hair for me was a legacy. Both

53

my grandmothers and my mother were all hairstylists. My mom was pregnant with me when she went to beauty school. Becoming a cosmetologist was second nature to me, just like swimming is second nature to the baby. I tell myself my mom knew I would be okay. She must have clearly saw something in me I did not see in myself. She had to throw me in that same pool of water as the baby, to see whether I would sink or swim. So yes, that was adversity for me most would sink in those circumstances. What I now realize looking back, that was probably the best way for my mom to set me up for success. Yes, I endured adversity, but in my mind, it was not adversity more than it was success.

I tell you that what I am going through right now writing this chapter is true pain for me. I could not see the light at the end of the tunnel while going through that situation with my mom. I find myself back in the same pain as I write now. For this pain to be caused by the industry I love is the worst pain for me. This pain is different. This pain caused me to question GOD, this pain has me questioning myself, this pain has me questioning my values. This pain for me, a person who never truly endured pain outside of my uncle and grandparents passing, is a totally different feeling. I continue to call on all my angels in heaven. I call on God. I call on friends and family, but receiving answers is seeming impossible. I continue to look at the words in my frame that reads "*Faith, Love, Hope*". Sometimes all you need is faith. Finding faith in the midst of this cloud seems to be almost impossible. I echo these words to myself:

You're unbreakable, you're selfless, you love this industry, and you believe in God, that's all you need.

Even if putting my truth out there means unimaginable pain. It is worth fighting for the industry I believe in. Then I questioned... but what is the truth? How do I write about the truth when there are two sides to every story? How do I write my truth when the truth really does not matter because law doesn't respect truth?

The law only respects law. Law by means: the system of rules which a particular country or community recognizes as regulating the actions of its members and which it may enforce by the imposition of penalties. Now let's take the secondary definition: a rule defining correct procedure or behavior in a sport. This definition doesn't identify by who's standards would correct procedures be considered? What does correct procedures even mean? How did one person or a team of people for that matter come up with correct procedures? What happened to make one come up with such rules? Were these rules written for us or to control us. Things happen in your life and sometimes they don't make much sense at all. It is not for you to try and figure it out because when you do you miss the message. Understanding having faith is believing even when the cloud is too thick to see through. Having faith is believing when all hope seems to be lost.

Let's take football for instance there was a time when players would catch the ball, run 100 yards without anyone touching them. They would even have to jump over other players who were knocked down while trying to get to them. They would outrun their counterpart. They would sometimes have to stiff arm a member of the opposing team then finally they would have to do a front flip to make it pass that small line to get in the in zone for the "TOUCHDOWN"! Now I want you to imagine you were playing football and you just did all of this to make it to and through that goal line. What feelings would you have? That same guy or gal would do all of that then celebrate with a major dance. At that moment, their adrenaline is pumping so hard the only thing they can do is dance it out. What is wrong with that behavior? It is a natural instinct to be excited about all the hurdles they had just overcome to make it that far. What happens now in the NFL is players are told you can celebrate but they limited the amount of time you can take to do so? They also limited the amount of energy they could exert in the other team face. You see this is the true definition of Law. The point I am trying to make is sometimes you are so excited about the success you have created. You are so excited about reaching the goal line, but then you're stopped by what someone other human being feels shouldn't happen. You are not allowed to dance, you are not allowed to celebrate, you are not allowed to be excited about the moment in history you just made.

The truth is the law was not created for us. The law was created to control us. I am sorry to tell you this industry was not created for us. One thing for sure and two things for certain we as the minority are talented individuals who know how to make a way out of no way. We are the ones with the natural rhythm that the law was made for in football. We were the ones dancing too much in the in zone. We are the ones who needed the law made to "keep us in our place".

It is said that the average American does not read books. Statistics show most Americans only read 1 book a year. This chapter was the chapter I needed to help pull me through. As I wrote this chapter, I was not in love with the industry, but I still loved what it does for others. I love how it makes others feel. The instant confidence builder one gets. The satisfaction of what this field does for others is what I am still in love with about this industry. Helping others is what we do. It is an industry of pleasing yourself through helping others. For me it is my duty, it is what God put me on this earth to do. The godly thing to do is to help others and this industry gives me the satisfaction of knowing that I am helping others and doing the godly thing. While I'm on this earth I want people to say she loved this industry so much she allowed it to beat her up but kept pushing and never quit. It is not about me and has never been about me. I do what I do to make sure my clients, my team, my children, my parents, and my husband are good. Your law will change a person. Law and order will make a difference so bad that it makes a person feel like you have no other option.

One day I thought let me go get a book to keep me encouraged. I purchased Joel Osteen book titled, *Blessed in the Darkness.* In the book, he says when God puts a dream in your heart, he will show you the beginning and the end. He will give you the promise, but he will not show you the middle. He goes on to say if he showed us all of it would take for our dream to come to pass, we would not stay on course.

It was important for me to add this here because I knew those words are true. I encourage you to stay on course. I know the path to your dreams is worth it. I have experienced what staying on course and not quitting will provide for you. Please push past your issues. Continue to dream your dream. Continue to live the dream you always wanted to conquer. Continue to bless others through the gift that God gave you. Continue to be the change not the chatter (words from my girl Nye). Continue to conquer and help others because like my friend Melissa told me the ones you are meant to help will love and appreciate the help. I had to understand: **You can't please everyone. You can't change anyone but YOU.**

I still believe I can conquer the world of cosmetology. Like Madame C.J. Walker, who used the beauty industry to become the first woman to become a self-made millionaire, quitting was never an option. She conquered the industry with products made for ethnic cultures. She did not stop until the world knew her name. Her name still resonates decades later. I say to you, do not let anything stop you from doing what you are meant to do no matter what others say or think. Go out there and triumph over everything and everyone (and all the naysayers). Make the world and all others believe just by the love you have for whatever it is you do.

> ### *Lesson 4*
>
> You won't please everyone
>
> You can't change anyone
>
> So start worrying about
>
> somebody...
>
> let that somebody be YOU!

Chapter 5:
COVID or Blackness

My dream caused unimaginable pain, yet it still was worth it. I became an owner of a beautiful salon, putting my blood sweat and tears into the very foundation of this place. I remember being in the building all night with contractor after contractor. Turning around saying if they cannot hang a chandelier, I will figure out how to hang it myself. If they want to charge an astronomical price, I will lay it myself. I'm talking about 1,300 square feet of straight ceramic porcelain tiles.

I asked my husband to lay these tiles because everyone was quoting me these very high prices. Seeing how it was killing me, he said "yes babe I'll do it". Then I came in one day after working at the salon to see him dead beat tired, no energy left in him. His knees burning and back weak. I said here babe I will help. Most times he said, "absolutely not I got it", but clearly this time his body would not allow those words to flow from his mouth.

Family and friends helping to add to the foundation.

Looking at the long floor and seeing he was 3 days in and only got maybe one third of the floor done. I took over with the help of my best friend and some other relatives. I called in an entire team of folks to help us lay this floor. After I laid about three rows, I quickly realized that all the rates I was being quoted were justified. I felt sorry for even putting my husband in this position. I continued to push past the back pain, knee pain, body aches, headaches and fatigue. This was all a part of my dream, and anything worth having is worth fighting for.

We finally got all the floors laid, walls put up, paint on walls, chandeliers hung, and televisions installed. The project I thought would take 2 months literally turned into an entire year. Let's not even talk about the many things the township put us through causing an additional year. Then to turn around and be shut down not able to do business because of COVID 19 (a major pandemic the world was facing) was devastating. When I tell you this dream was causing me so much heartache, I mean it. Heartache, backache etc. not just physical but mental drainage! Why, because God didn't show me the middle. He put all these thoughts of how magnificent everything would be. He surely did not tell me it would take three years.

Contractor after contractor, and thousands of dollars with no monetary help. God provides! However, I continued to push past the limits, and barriers to hit another roadblock. COVID-19 had finally let up (so we thought) Governor Murphy said salons and barbershops can now open, we opened in our new salon a 6,200 square foot facility, and boy was it beautiful! The doors opened! To see the reaction on clients' faces as they walked through the doors was priceless. It became all worthwhile. The long nights, draining contractor conversations and money was all worth it. We opened our doors and boy was it great. Client after client packed schedules, tons of money floating through and great vibes. One of my long-term goals was coming into fruition before my very eyes.

Prior to the shutdown of COVID 19, I submitted all my paperwork to the state, about 7 months before the shutdown. We heard nothing back from them. We reached out a multitude of times through calls, e-mails, certified letters, you name it we did it. Day after day, month after month, years leading into another year nothing, I was mad

Meeting with the director of NJ State Board of Cosmetology when we submitted our application in 2019

as hell, it was like they were ignoring us purposely. I figured okay maybe because of COVID we were not getting any answers. I assumed once they opened back up from COVID they would finally push things through, so I opened our doors. I figured God would guide my footsteps.

My sister put up a post on social media with pictures of the salon and school which read "*The first black owned and operated cosmetology school in New Jersey enrolling now*". Although I thought, no we're not ready yet, it was too late the post had already gone viral. Hundreds of calls were coming in. There were thousands of hits to our website causing the website to crash. The response was so overwhelming I thought this had to be nothing but "the Grace of God".

We opened our website for the salon and even that was a flood of clients needing their hair done after waiting months not being able to receive any services thanks to COVID 19. Thanking God day after day and hour after hour, another one of my goals had come to fruition. Then we got word the state finally opened and we were on their line again day after day. They finally approved us for the first 2 steps in the approval process then we got to the last step which was the inspection. When this lady came in, I could see the jealousy all over her face the blatant disrespect wondering, how did these "blacks" do this. If this was not what she was thinking her energy and questions surely showed it. She came in with an American flag bandanna wrapped around her face. She made statements like "if you're going to register convicts, they have to sit before the board first". It was like she was insinuating that because we were black, we were going to do all things illegal. That encounter did not end well, and I felt attacked and discriminated against. She left and did not leave us any report after looking at the place multiple times. It was my understanding that whenever an inspector inspected anything they should leave some type of formal document letting you know their findings. Well, we did not receive any documentation.

Time went on, we waited for months more after already waiting for years to find out whether we were approved for the third step or denied. Finally, after waiting months and reaching out to every power that be in our network (including the governor himself) we received "the letter".

NJ Governor Phil Murphy with my son DJ

A letter that had minor details but one major issue. It was like this letter was an attack on my entire character. With everything in the letter, the only thing, I read that stood out big and bold was **CEASE AND DESIST**. They were not just trying to time us out at this point, the State was also trying to stop our money flow, so we could not continue to keep our doors open. Most people would tell me, well you cannot say they were discriminating against you. It will just seem like you're just another little black girl shouting, "*it's because I'm black!*" Even my lawyer (which I quickly fired) told me well you do not really have a case, you must be able to prove malicious intent. It is funny when black people are being treated wrong, we do not get to bitch and complain. When any other nationality is being treated wrong, they can bitch, and moan and the world just allows it. They are not told you must show malicious intent. As if proving negligence with all the paper trail we kept was not enough. As if sending certified letters of which someone clearly had to sign to receive yet still not getting a reply was not enough. Filing tort claims still was not enough.

Do you honestly think I'm the first person in my state who thought about opening a black owned and operated school? Maybe I am, I just refuse to believe it. What I believe is the state never wanted that to happen. Doing something to help the advancement of our people was never in the equation. They said little black girl who do you think you are? Trying to step outside of the boundaries we are allowing. I do not know if many others had the fight in them and just threw in the towel, but it surely was not an option for me.

You see, this dream I had was just a dream to me. It was something I heard my parents, the wealthy, my guidance counselors, people on television and radio say, "Dream Big". I had a dream to help colored people learn the cosmetology trade without having to go in debt to do it. I had a dream to help people get licensed in a trade to start making money to feed their families right out of school. Many schools only teach people how to pass the test. They never teach how to pass the industry test. I had a dream to help! I did not realize this dream would cause so much hate. I did not realize this dream would cause so much pain and confusion.

Many nights I asked God "why?", as I write these words, I'm still asking God "Why?" I asked God, "Why did you bring me this far only to leave me here?" I thought God was ordering my steps. I thought God made the post go viral. I thought God was at the center of all of this. I just could not see how God could possibly be at the center of mayhem. God helped me get every penny to be able to pay every contractor and get every piece of material, then snatched it all away. I said God you brought me into this world and guided my parents to give me the very name "Atiya" (which means a beautiful gift from God). Yet. when I'm trying to be that gift to others it all gets snatched away. My dream that's worth living was causing me to question God in ways I never imagined I would have to question Him. I would ask God night after night, "What is this? What am I supposed to do? What am I supposed to learn? What am I missing? Many nights I would ask these questions to get no response. I would talk to my friends, clients, husband, listen to my bishop.

All I kept hearing was have faith, but how could I have faith when I thought God was ordering my steps all along to find out they were not the steps I should have taken. In all of it, God was not talking to me at all. Well, He would throw little signs to remind me I have a gift and I need to keep going. I am tired, beat up and beat down. I have children, clients, students, employees, friends all counting on me as a leader to make this dream come true. How can I do that if I can no longer hear God and everything that is happening day by day is just more bad news. I asked God many nights to let up off me, I can't take it anymore. However, the foot and heavy weight remained planted right on my neck.

I started listening and reading many books. I knew this could not have been what God wanted for me. I knew there was more in store for me. I knew the pain I was feeling could not last for always. Every time I would say to myself, *"I'm done I can't take it anymore"*, God would send me an angel to remind me your journey is not over. Going through this pain had to be for me to help someone else. Going through this pain had to mean greater was coming! Most times when you want to give up know that you are right at the edge of greater on the other side.

If you are a female, you'll understand what I am about to say. If you have ever been pregnant and went through delivering a child, you know those last seconds are probably some of the worst pains you have ever felt. As you went through the entire process the more you started to dilate, the harder the contractions got. You went from 5 cm to 6 cm, 7 cm to 8, cm 9 cm and right at 9 cm you started to feel the worst pain in life. As if 9 cm was not hard enough, you finally get to 10 for it to get worse and worse and worse. Then a miracle finally happens, you push this beautiful baby out. You begin to send the praises up for this blessing God has bestowed upon you. Realizing this is the blessing. In all the pain, being worth it is a true understatement.

I kept hearing, keep pushing, keep taking one step at a time because as long as you take one, God will take two. Everything does not happen the way you want it to happen. You will go through things in life and sometimes you don't understand why you are going through it, but I promise you if you keep pressing forward all will change. This test will turn into a testimony. Your story will continue to bless someone else. God will continue to bless you. Greatness does not happen without trials and tribulations. If you want to be a name, the nation will remember. Do you want to be a name that stands in the history books? If you want to be a Martin Luther King, Malcolm X, Tupac, Madame C.J. Walker, Harriet Tubman, you must be willing to put your big girl pants on and go into the battlefield because life is not easy. If you want to live a life other than average...it is time for you to fight!

Walking into a disaster that I knew would turn into a diamond.

Before the vision came together

*One of many conversations with our plumber trying to
understand what in the world he was talking about.*

Standing where it started.

Dwayne getting busy while laying the floors.

One of many Home Depot runs.

The vision that is reality.

Chapter 6:
Commit First

I encourage you to go into any job, career, or business and give it 110 percent. When you do this, you will love what you do even more, and the payoff will be much more worth it. I say needed another job is for quitters not to offend anyone but to say if you give whatever your current situation is 110 you should not need another especially in the beauty industry. I have hired so many people that felt like they had to leave working at the salon to go do 2-3 hours at a part time job to make $16 an hour. Since I love breaking down the math let's do it again. You come into the salon from 9-3 which is 6 hours.

Let's say you do 1 weave for $160; this takes 2 hours you, then have 1 relaxer client for $65 which takes 1 ½ hours. After that, you follow that up with 3 wash and curls at $45 each which takes the remainder of your 6 hours. Understand these are low numbers and most stylists that give 110 percent will kill this math in 1-2 hours on one service, let alone 5. That total for those services would give you $360. You finish that shift then leave to go to your part time gig for 3 hours at $16 an hour which gives you $48 for that day (which taxes will clearly take $20). Now let's do the weekly math. If a stylist completed this same process each day (which does not normally happen because some days you will do and make more and sometimes less) their weekly total would be $1800 in salon pay, and only $240 for the week in second gig/part time job pay. Does it still make sense to waste these hours for part-time pay or stay at the salon a little longer?

I came into the salon this day to look at my schedule. What seemed like it would be a very busy day turned out to be a very busy day (you probably thought I typed that wrong). Yes, I meant a very busy day. The fact that the day was busy was not the issue for me because any successful stylist understands busy days every day is what you must strive for. If you're not there yet, I want you to become that person in the salon that is there first and leaving last. Of course, I want you to be busy all day not just sitting around waiting for someone to call or enter. If you're not quite there yet, I still want you to come first and leave last. You should be the person shadowing everything the top producing stylist is doing. I want you to home in on their attitude, their style, the way they speak to their clients, the way they dress, the way they listen, the way they see everything happening around them. For this field to ever be the only job/life, you see for yourself you must mimic all the good habits of everyone currently doing it. I promise you once you start to visually see exactly what that person is doing you will be able to either mimic them or do better than them (which is what I want for you).

This particular day meant so much to me because at a time where I was starting to lose hope for the industry this client reminded me (without knowing) of the importance of having people like me in their world. She was my first client of the day, when she called to schedule an appointment, she was very adamant about not wanting to get her hair washed. She only wanted us to straighten her hair. I will be honest, in my salon we do not particularly like this scenario because clients usually do not shampoo to our liking. My administrative assistant must have felt that this woman really needed to be seen. I'm not sure exactly what the conversation was over the phone between the client and my AA, but she squeezed her in on my schedule to be the first person I would touch that day. You see God has a way of making things happen in your life that even you do not know you need at the time. I was amid writing this book for all stylists of the world, but I was going through turmoil in my life causing me to start to self-doubt. Then God sent an angel for me to be able to continue to be an angel for you and let you know "You are where you are supposed to be". I came into the salon really early this day. My main stylist and manager were out, so I had to be the person to open up. The woman comes in, checks in at the front desk, sits down and waits for me as I finish scarfing down my breakfast (all my stylist buddies understand this word "scarf down" lol), then I proceed to get her started. As she sits in my chair, the first thing she asked was "did I wash my hair correctly"? I looked through her scalp, by my surprise she actually did do a great job on her shampoo. As I assessed her hair, I noticed she had very healthy hair that was left untouched by a true professional for some time. Her hair was not very damaged, but it did have some damage that could definitely be fixed with some tender love, care, and treatments. As I started her hair, she began to tell me how her old stylist stopped doing hair over a year and a half prior to this day, because she was going through some family issues. She told me she had sent almost 40 different referrals to this stylist but the lady just up and left. All the referrals she sent the stylist started calling her asking who is going to do our hair now? She said they were upset with her because she referred them, and they ended up in a vulnerable state. She began telling me how this stylist was perfect for all of them. She took care of their hair, treated them well, got them out of the salon in a timely manner, and did it all for a very reasonable price. When I am finished with this story, I'll show and tell you why pricing is never an issue you should ever worry about.

"Atiya, I feel so vulnerable," the woman said, "I am not myself. My husband is tired of me looking like this, but I just don't know what I'm going to do". Those were her exact words that hit me like a ton of bricks. As she proceeded to go on and on about her old stylist, her husband, the clients that became upset with her and so forth, I was stuck on that one line--"*I feel so vulnerable*"!

For me that line was the line that told me enough is enough this woman is sitting in your chair telling you she feels so vulnerable it's almost bringing her to tears. Many of you reading this book may not understand, but some will get it.

To the people who get it you already understand! To the ones who are saying "girl please stop its just your hair" --- Let me explain to you why it's so much more than just your hair. A person's hair is an outward appearance of their feelings. A person's hair is the very thing that gives them the confidence to be able to go into the world with the confidence they need for the day. I am going to a make a bold statement here. A person's hair is on the same level as a person's wallet. The confidence that money gives you when you go into the world is the same confidence your hair gives you when you go into the world. Guy or girl, it does not matter, we all can agree with this. When you leave out your house, you are broke and cannot put gas in your car... how much confidence do you really have? Doesn't that put you in a vulnerable state? When you must ask someone to borrow money so you can put gas in your car, that makes you feel very vulnerable.

This client, and many others feel this same vulnerability if their hair isn't right, and let's not even talk about your hair not being right for years. For her it was her hair. For you it could be money. No matter what it is that puts you in a state of vulnerability it changes the very fabric of who you are. So yes, that line hit me differently because in that moment I became the person to help bring her out of that vulnerable place. It's the same feeling you get when you give a homeless person money. Whether they use the money to buy food or not you still feel like you helped them be a little less vulnerable. I didn't care whether she came back to me or not it was more important for me to help her in that moment. I continued styling her hair never to attempt to sell her on me becoming her permanent stylist. For me it was not about trying to persuade her because I totally understood what she had been through. She told me she finally started going to another stylist to get color and that lady tore her hair up while everyone in the salon sat and watched, Then the stylist left while she had color on her hair and told the owner to finish the clients hair (instead of saying I don't know how to achieve this from the beginning). Attempt after attempt she tried to give stylist after stylist a chance to bring her out of the uncomfortable place in her hair life but was unsuccessful.

The definition of vulnerable: **susceptible to physical or emotional attack or harm. (Of a person) in need of special care, support, or protection because of age, disability, or risk of abuse or <u>neglect.</u>**

Said client was neglected for whatever the reason was. Everything happens for a reason if this client would not have been neglected by someone at some point, she wouldn't have been able to be my angle in that moment. I was not happy she was neglected, however I needed to hear her voice and story that day to help me. Sometimes we don't even realize we need help, but God has a way of putting people and things in your life to help solidify your calling.

Lesson 6

1. Think about a time you felt vulnerable. Write down a time you helped someone out of vulnerability.

_____

_____

2. Have you had a person come into your life who has helped you realize your Gift? What is that gift and how can you share it with the world?

_____

_____

_____

Now let's do the math...

3. How many people can you share your gift with that will help you make your next million?

_____

_____

_____

Chapter 7:
You Are Where You Should Be

I had many stylist works for me that didn't understand that they were blessed into hair. You may be reading this and asking yourself how in the world can a person be blessed into hair? Society would tell you the beauty industry is nothing to brag about. I am telling you I have been in places and thought to myself maybe I should do something else. Maybe this industry is not all it is cracked up to be. Yet every time I seemed to have that very thought God would send me a clear sign telling me "This is for you". Every Successful person will tell you, the stage that brings you to your destiny is generally unknowingly and uncomfortable. I'm not saying the beauty industry is your ultimate purpose, but it could be the point that brings you closer to what God has for you. It is ultimately your blessing. It could very well be the point of reference that affords you the life needed to see your mission through.

I know if you are in this industry, there has been many times you questioned is this really all I need? Is my talent as great as the greats in this industry? You've probably asked yourself at times what am I doing wrong that I can't get a picture, a video, something to go viral so people would know who I am. These are all questions I asked myself. I'm here to tell you like my Uncle G (Grant Cardone that is) told me; "you don't have to do it the best you just have to be the best known. When I heard him say that in a *10X Bootcamp* I thought he's 100% right. Many of the greats in the industry are not the best in it, they just put themselves in a position to be the best known in the industry. Whether that means they posted on social media everyday 3 times a day. Maybe they used filters on all their pictures to have the pictures look more polished. Maybe they had an opportunity to do celebrity work and they seize the opportunity. One thing they did was stayed consistent, and finally had a big break. You see, these are things you can do as well, these folks just knew every opportunity they got to make this thing better they would do it.

Listen to me when I say the moment you put a thought into the universe, and you start to take actionable steps to see the process through God will move you to where you need to be. Do not start thinking maybe the beauty industry is not for me because I cannot get a viral video to save my life. Instead of that thought, think what I can do to get a viral video and take actionable steps to make it happen. If that means you must post every 10 seconds a day, do it and don't feel bad about it. I guarantee you one of those videos is going to make something shake. Do not start thinking maybe I should become a nurse because I cannot get a famous person to allow me to do their hair. Think God I would really love to get into celebrity hair please order my steps. God rewards non quitters! The people who do everything in their power to make their dreams come true God rewards. If you decide I think it is time for me to throw in the towel without giving this industry your all, that's quitting.

You choose this industry for a reason and if god helped you get through however many months or years (depending on your state) schooling, graduate, pass the test (which is not an easy task), land a gig you were blessed into this industry. Let's not even talk about if you're the stylist with raw talent. In other words, if you can take a canvas (client) and just create a masterpiece without even knowing where you were going, that's raw talent. If you're the person in the salon everyone is coming in asking for, a Genuine spirit, or a willingness to make everyone happy you probably have raw talent.

When you're doing what you are supposed to be doing God will make it very clear for you. As I was writing this book I was going through a major setback in my life. I began to ask myself and God what is all of this. I did not know why I was going through any of the trials and tribulations I was facing. However, one thing about me is I do not quit!

My dad instilled this philosophy in me at a very young age. In our karate school we use to say this word "Os" it means keep going strong and never give up. Whenever I went in my life and career whenever I had just a minuscule thought of giving up, I would say to myself "Os". At any rate giving up wasn't an option and so as I went through the trials, I would begin to ask God, *why.*

I would start dousing myself in different motivational and biblical books. As I read these books the message across the board was, *when you're at the edge of giving up just over that cliff is your breakthrough.* Just over your cliff is greatness. Just over that cliff is success beyond measures. Do not be afraid to walk all the way to the end of the cliff, when you walk off God is going to give you wings to fly. You will not have to worry about plunging to your death because god is ordering those steps.

For everyone step you take God is taking two. He is making sure he always remained in front of you, right over that edge he's there to make you walk over water. He is there to give you wings. As I was going through these trails god would give me small yet big signs telling me you're in the right place. You are doing the right thing.

I was never a fan of surgery; I am sure you are not either lol. I have had a hernia for years I lived with pain and a huge bulge in my belly for 15 years. I ended up going out on surgery leave for 3 weeks. Prior to those 3 weeks, I signed up for this Grant Cardone Live Interactive bootcamp which date fell on the first week of my surgery leave. Honestly, because I was so petrified of surgery my intention was never to get it done. I scheduled the appointment, but I planned to cancel it the closer to the date it got. When I scheduled the initial appointment, I could have sworn the date was April 15th, but the scheduler from the surgeon office called me on March 31st checking to see if I got the preliminary task done. I asked her, "Wait, when is my surgery?" She replied, "you're scaring me Mrs. Johnson your procedure is scheduled for Monday April 5th". At this moment, I could not cancel. She was so nice it was almost like God moved the date up to force me to get the procedure done. I talked to my girlfriend, and she said go and get the surgery done you need the time off to regroup. She was 100% right. I was so worried that my clients, my business, my children, everyone needed me to continue to work yet the truth was they needed me to sit down and take the time so I could be the best version of myself for them. I didn't cancel the surgery. I had my administrative assistant call all my scheduled people to change to a different day or move their appointment to another stylist. As my bishop always says, "stay with me I'm going to bless you". I got the surgery done on Monday. That Friday was the grant Cardone bootcamp. I would not have made if not for the surgery. My schedule for that weekend was swamped with clients, although the bootcamp was live I would had never been free enough to take in all the goodness.

Whenever I listen to Grant, read one of his books, or attend one of his conferences, my career and thought process takes off to another level. Day 1 of the conference we would have breakout sessions, to network and have conversation with like-minded individuals. When I tell you God orders your steps, it is the God's honest truth. He is going to make sure you are aware of if you are in the right place at the right time. See sometimes you may not be going viral because God knows you are not ready for it. You may not be doing celebrity hair because God wants you to soar to the next level. He must prepare you and build your confidence so when you're in their presence you will seize the moment! Grant's team put us into our first breakout room, but before they moved us, Jarred president of Grant Cardone's company said, "the person that is to talk first is the person with the longest hair". If you did not get that yet, beauty is everywhere! Hair is everywhere, Grant's team had to use hair as the thing to keep 10,000 people in order. He could have said the person with the darkest shirt. He could have said the person with the smallest nose. There were many things he could have used to keep us in line, but he used hair. Not to mention it was the first indication for me that I was in the right place at the right time. He went on to say the person with the shortest hair keeps time to keep you all on track. We enter our breakout rooms and it's two people with the same length of hair. It was me and another lady named "Jana". I didn't pay attention to her name on her screen, so I never realized what her name was until she started talking. She and I discussed whose hair was longer, but I said to her "looks like you got this one" (laughing). I then went to write her name down in my "networking people's" book, then I felt God hit me in my forehead. The name of my business is "Jana's" it's the name my mom chose which stands for Jamal, Atiya, Nasir, Ayanna (her four children's name). It is a legacy name that I even pondered changing for a moment.

I didn't change it, because my entire purpose has always been to make sure my mom's legacy will go down in the history books. If what happened hasn't hit, you yet like it didn't hit me allow me to reintroduce what happened. I, Atiya Johnson essentially told my Empire (Jana's), "looks like you got this one". Now please allow me to put this into perspective for you in case you're not following where I'm going. God moved my surgery date (my best friend would say I got the date wrong from the beginning, but I like God moved it), placed me in a bootcamp to launch me to the next level.

All the while, God made sure I understand I was in the right place at the right time. by making the first person who spoke in my training group have the name of my empire that I am continuing to build to levels beyond my imagination. You cannot tell me my God isn't real!

I am saying this to say your journey is not over until God says it is over. Do not give up on your dreams, and damn sure do not give up on the beauty industry! Your time is now. Go out there and seize your moment. Do not let anyone define what success looks like for you. Talk to God, walk with God, and believe in God and all things through him are achievable! I pray I encouraged you to see the great in this industry or whatever industry you are involved. These rules apply to life. If you are a beauty professional, I am your sister in prosperity! If you are in another industry, I'm still your sister in prosperity!

My journey sure isn't over, and yours isn't either. Live your life to please God and great things will happen in your life! You are where you are for reasons greater than you can imagine, so walk the walk and talk the talk but always do it with God and cosmetology in mind!

Lesson 7

Think of a time in your life that you started doing something other than what you knew was right for you? Write down below what you should have done in that moment.

Is there something in your life now that you should be doing differently? If yes, explain.

_____

_____

_____

_____

Think about a time you felt under-supported by someone who mattered most to you. What have/will you do to use that person to push you closer to success?

_____

_____

_____

_____

Chapter 8:
Execution is Kueen

Kueen: a woman making king moves, who has ambitions and drive ready to execute by any means Necessary. It is my job to get you to execute after reading this book. I want you to execute like a king or a Kueen. Do not "just" take this book and read it. Figure out how will you change your life at this very moment then execute.

If you are just a hairstylist right now what else can you do to take the next step. Maybe that's creating your own line of products. Maybe that means you are setting a goal to make a million this year. It is easy. It is all doable. You must do the math. If that means you have always wanted to work in that one salon in your area, but you have been scared to reach out to the owner...do it anyway and do it NOW! Stop reading, go make the call and simply say, "Are you hiring"? I've been following you for a long time and I've finally built the confidence to reach out and ask you to hire me. I guarantee you they are hiring and would love to have you be part of their team. If you are procrastinating to start that salon. Stop reading, go find a realtor to help you find a business location. Take the first step now! Do not wait, do it anyway even if you don't have the money now. Learn what's needed then figure out how much money it takes to make it happen. Commit first then figure the rest out (grant Cardone). Understand there are reasons people do not execute. Whether those reasons are fear, not knowing what steps to take, procrastination or a lack of belief, you must make the first step then I promise you God with stand all around you to push you forward. Making sure he puts you in the right places at the right time!

I wrote this and kept it short because I want you to start to execute. I do not want you to dabble in the industry I want you to go all in. I want you and I to rush to the finish line together. You must be fully invested and if you can't figure it out on your own, join forces with someone who is doing more than you. Get behind someone and be willing to grow and advance. Success loves speed, don't wait, don't procrastinate, change your life now. Change your mind now. Change your philosophy so you can start to execute on what you know is important.

You must quit waiting and be enthusiastic about taking the next step. If you do not know whether it's going to work or not, don't think about it "Do it anyway"! Understand that what you are doing now isn't working so let's flip things and do it anyway. The information most Americans currently have is the very reason American is in such a bad place. It is within your best interest to pick someone to study and stay with them. Just make sure it is a mentor who will force you to execute!

All our lives we had conflicting information. Bad information that may have come from the government, your parents, your friend, family etc. This conflicting information is causing you massive amounts of money and information. The longer you take to press forward, you are losing money by the minutes. The reason most people cannot make a sound decision is because they are constantly thinking what would my such and such think.

We are constantly worried what effect would our decisions have on others. My friend knew she was tired of her engineer job and needed a change. She executed, changed paths, and opened her own business. Before you start thinking I'm telling you to go open your own business I'm not. You can be just as successful working with someone else in their salon. My best friend Latisee is a very loyal person and has been with our company for 20 plus years. She understands that as I continue to succeed that success will also follow her. She knows her loyalty and determination has been paying off and will continue. Opening her own salon was not an interest of hers. Some people are made to be great builders. I consider her to be a builder. She is one that will put her all into the very foundation until it explodes. Her only interest was helping to push the business to a point of success of which she knew I would eventually make happen. I am an owner who wants to see everyone on her team win. If I am a millionaire, everyone on my team are also millionaires.

Take me for instance, when my mother had her breakdown, I wasn't excited to take over her spot it was important for me to make sure my mom's legacy could live on forever. A wise man once told me before you can be a great leader you have to be a great follower. I was honored to follow my mom. When the time arose for me to step up, I did the best I could. Although I am an owner, I still live to make sure my mom's legacy will never die. My mom was faithful to the beauty industry, I feel it is my duty to make sure she reaps the benefits of her hard work. Whether you choose to follow a leader to greatness, open your own salon or be a legacy builder just EXECUTE!

When I was younger many people would say to me "Are you going to be a hairstylist like your mom"? My answer "No". I never wanted to be a stylist because I saw the long hours my mom would work. The only thing I saw at a young age was my mom was always working and not home. You see those long work hours to a kid seemed like an eternity. She would make us breakfast, OMG my mom makes the best pancakes. Those pancakes are so light and fluffy with crispy edges. "Bring it back Atiya", I just had to reminisce about those pancakes paired with delicious apple sauce. It was the breakfast for champs. She would send us off to school after breakfast and most days we wouldn't see her until the next morning. I didn't understand it as a kid but as an adult I totally get it. I'm more like my mom then I ever thought I would be. She has such a genuine spirit everyone loves her which makes it very hard for her to say No. Often time she was at the salon late not only because of her love for the industry but her willingness to make sure every client was taken care of. She is the definition of an obsessed stylist.

Although life's obstacles got in the way she put her all into this industry and it rubbed off on me.

Lesson 8

What does the word "execution" mean to you?

_____

_____

_____

What has procrastination done for you in the past?

_____

_____

_____

What can execution do for you today?

_____

_____

_____

Lesson 8 (continued)

Name 3 steps you will take...

1. Commit to: *waking up early everyday.*

    _____

    _____

    _____

2. Understand my: *blessing is important to share with the rest of the world.*

    _____

    _____

    _____

3. Start to execute by: *writing m goals down every night before I go to bed.*

    _____

    _____

    _____

Chapter 9:
A Pioneer

As I continue to go through my journey, I make a conscious decision to listen and take heed to God's signs and His voice. While driving to the Atlantic City Airport this day to pick up my husband, something happened that made me change my perspective and outlook. Prior to this day I started reading a book (well listening to it on Audible) called, "The Obstacle is The Way" By Ryan Holiday. I realized I needed to start listening to some encouraging books to keep my mind in a stable yet growing condition. As I'm driving to pick up Dwayne from the airport, I was listening to the chapter titled, "The Process".

In this section, he talks about focusing on following the process and not the price. He proceeds to talk about understanding that you need to think about surviving instead of thinking about the end. He goes on to say dealing with the steps within the process is more important than trying to figure out the steps. In essence, he was telling me don't try to look at the full picture (which is something that was going through heavy during this time). He said if I continue to look at the entire process I'll get paralyzed and will not do anything. I truly felt he was talking directly to me at this point. It's what happened next that made me realize I was supposed to be listening to this part of this book while driving to get Dwayne. This moment was already written in God's plan for me. In the next, chapter he starts to talk about Amelia Earhart. Prior to this book the only other time I heard about Amelia Earhart was in a Jay-Z rap. Maybe I did hear about her in history class but wasn't paying attention. Who knows?

At any rate he starts about her by saying "Amelia Earhart wanted to be a great Aviator, but it was the 1920 and people still thought that women were frail and weak and didn't have the stuff. Women suffrage wasn't even a decade old". He went on to talk about how she was given an offensive proposition for her to fly a plane, but would not get paid to do so and may die in the interim.

As I continue to drive while listening to this part of the book on the accomplishments of Amelia Earhart, my GPS tells me to make a left onto Amelia Earhart Blvd. I thought to myself "wait a minute what just happened here"? Let me repeat the book is talking to me about Amelia Earhart while the GPS tells me to turn onto Amelia Earhart Blvd. I don't know if you're like me or not, but I like to take heed to the signs and signals that are in front of me. Only God could arrange for these steps to happen. I could've been listening to any other book, but I was listening to this book. At that very moment, the GPS tells me to make a left on the same named road. I proceeded to start talking to myself. "Wow, what just happened? Who is this Amelia Earhart and why did you want me to hear about her at this time GOD"? I picked Dwayne up and as soon as he got in the car I asked, "Babe, who is Amelia Earhart"? He answered with "she's the first woman to ever fly a plane across the Atlantic Ocean. I don't even think I said hey babe how was your trip. I proceeded to tell him what had just happened, but of course he didn't give me the energy I was seeking.

Normally when things like that happen I call one of my girlfriends because men just don't understand. I thought to myself I need him to drive so I can do my research on this woman. However, he was too tired to drive so I didn't mention it I just kept driving. As the day went on, I went to church and didn't think any more about it until I left out of church. When I'm in church I must be present in that moment so I can fully receive the word God is giving to me.

After I left out of church, I do my normal routine and call Devon. She like to live vicariously through me as it pertains to church. Every Sunday after service I call her, and we discuss what the message of the day was that Bishop gave. I proceeded to tell her the Amelia Earhart story. Devon is a researcher. She's the type of person who is doing the research as you're talking without you even asking her too (hints why she was voted most likely to succeed in school).

As I'm talking and telling her the story she's researching. She says, "Yeah, I remember going over her story in history class, but you probably don't remember because you were always sleeping." She's not lying I slept a lot in class, but still managed to get Honor roll. Nevertheless, she says Tia listen to this. "Amelia Earhart disappeared in 1937." I said, "okay and what does that mean"? She said, "Tia flip those numbers around." I stopped and thought about what she just said. Things go over my head frequently. Then it hit me...I said 1937 flipped around a bit is 1397 the address to the building we are leasing which is housing The First Black owned and operated Cosmetology school in New Jersey. She went a step further and said she was born on July 24th You formed Jana's Cosmetology Academy on July 23rd. At that moment things got very real for me. I realized God wanted me to hear her name for reasons deeper than just a name. I began to recite the Serenity prayer in my head at that moment. I don't know why I was saying this prayer but for some reason it was the first thing that came to my head after these findings.

God grant me the Serenity to accept the things I cannot change, the Courage to change the things I can, and the Wisdom to know the Difference.

Like Amelia who developed a passion for adventure at a young age, I developed a passion for the beauty industry at a young age. She became the first female to accomplish a task that was far from easy. I'm becoming the first black female owner of a cosmetology school in New Jersey. In an industry that is owned by predominately Caucasian men, I am up against a war I didn't even realize I was entering. I'm sure there are women reading this book who were born to be wild, born to be innovative, born to be a go getter, and born to fight until you get what you deserve. This world we live in is not fair, but if you're a woman you are already at odds. We were born into the wilderness. For us to make it out of the wilderness and prosper, we will have to fight a battle we probably never saw coming, just like Amelia. I use the word "born" loosely because what I really mean is even in the conception stage the odds are supposed to be stacked against us. Throughout the years I've learned that women are not incapable. Society conditions us to believe men represent strength while women are viewed as inferior. When in fact from conception we are tenacious and persistent. Let's dig into just a tad bit of science here. The male produces two different types of sperm. Female sperm i.e. X chromosomes and Male sperm I.E. Y chromosome. Female sperm is slow yet thicker than male sperm, which means it's going to take longer to get to the egg. Male sperm is fast and thinner, which means it's going to beat the female sperm to the egg. However, The fact that female sperm is slow and thick, it allows the male sperm to try and fertilize the egg quicker. Yet at the same time it will often die off because it can't withstand the harsh acidic environment of the female system. While the male sperm is dying off the female sperm which is moving slow (allowing all the others to die off) is so powerful it withstands the harsh environment. Ladies if you haven't heard before now let me be the first to tell you,...You are powerful. you are strong, and most importantly you must continue to be relentless.

God wanted me to hear this message so whenever I thought about giving up, I would think about Amelia Earhart and women struggles from conception to demise.

You see all I want to do is create a space for underserved individuals to be able to thrive at an affordable cost while being unstoppable in their industry. Like Amelia she didn't realize she would be met with such defeat for simply being a woman. Maybe God wanted me to hear this message and her story so I would understand nothing worth having will ever come easy. Maybe he wanted to give me a sign that I am on the right track by bringing the year of her death and the address of our building to the light. Only God knows what he's doing however I believe the dots in your life are meant to connect. God will give you signs that suggest maybe you should go a certain direction. It's up to you to decide if you'll be a great follower of whatever higher power, you believe in.

My client sent me a meme that read: People want to take your spot, until they realize what it takes to play your position! People who are good at what they do always make it look easy! I would go on to say God makes it look easy but sometimes he will you with some adversity and trails to test your courage and see if you really want it.

One thing that people who defy the odds have in common is they get started. Blowing through gender stereotypes is something Amelia had to do to get started. What matters is that we take the risk and get started. Don't feel sorry for yourself. Take the opening and press ahead. Don't fear taking action and pressing ahead. Get started get moving. Commit first and figure the rest out later. Take the bat off your shoulder and give it a hit. Put your full effort in everything you do. Be a curse breaker, and break through every devil that stands in your path.

My story continues and yours will too as long as you get and stay in the game. If you get started, you have nothing to lose. Do nothing and nothing happens. Do something to receive what's coming. Life isn't a crystal stair trust me. I will tell you success doesn't come easy, and you may piss the devil, the naysayer, and the haters off but as long as you continue to press forward GOD will have your back. Stay focused on forward movement and take one step at a time. If you take the first step God will guide you to continue taking the rest of the steps. Stay Blessed, stay encouraged, but most importantly Stay Focused!!!!!!

Lesson 9

Who is in charge of your GPS?

_____

Are you "listening" to your GPS?

_____

Where is your GPS directing you to go?

_____

_____

Afterword

These are some messages I heard going through my journey that I think may bless you as you go through yours.

Your battle is your Bridge, you cannot find your gift without a battle. ---TD Jakes

You'll be ill-equipped for the battle, but as long as you have confidence and God nothing else matters.
---TD Jakes

Your network equals your net worth.
---Grant Cardone

The battle is not yours it belongs to the Lord.

--- 2 Chronicles 20:15

The odds can be against you, but if God be for you, no man will stop you.

---Romans 8:31

The problem is your promise; therefore, you will become relevant because of the problem.

---Ryan Holiday

Nice is good, and nice is wonderful, but you better have some fight in you to win the battle.

---TD Jakes

God is going to create problems that makes your gift IMPORTANT!

---Dr. Myles Munroe

Man looks at the outer appearance, but God looks at the Heart.

---Bishop Robinson of Yesha Ministries

Your enemy will always dishevel your emotions, don't let him take you off your course.

---Atiya Johnson

APPENDIX

100 Affirmations

What you say out of your mouth and in your mind is powerful! Re write these affirmations and use them daily to speak power in your daily life.

1. I love myself.

_____

2. I am loved.

_____

3. I am capable of love.

_____

_____

4. I am worthy of happiness.

_____

_____

5. I am resilient.

_____

6. I am beautiful inside and out.

_____

_____

7. I am brave.

_____

8. I am happy.

_____

9. I am strong.

_____

10. I am capable.

_____

11. I am worthy.

_____

12. I am supportive to my own dreams.

_____

_____

13. I am a dreamer.

_____

14. I am a "goal" digger.

_____

15. I am a great friend.

_____

16. I am not ashamed.

_____

17. I will use my fear as fuel to overcome anything.

----

18. I will welcome joy to my life.

----

19. I am willing to grow.

----

20. I am willing to change for the best.

----

21. I believe in myself.

_____

_____

22. I trust myself.

_____

23. I will learn from my past and look toward the future.

_____

_____

24. I deserve love.

_____

25. I deserve happiness.

_____

26. I am becoming the best version of myself.

_____

_____

27. I am looking forward.

_____

28. I have the power.

_____

29. I can learn from my mistakes.

_____

30. I will achieve my goals.

_____

31. I can create great things.

_____

_____

32. I will take advantage of every positive opportunity.

_____

_____

33. I will think positively.

_____

_____

34. I am calm.

_____

35. I am bold.

_____

36. I deserve to be heard.

_____

_____

37. I believe my opinion is valuable.

----

38. I believe my potential is limitless.

----

39. I can manifest my biggest dreams.

----

40. I will not apologize for putting myself first.

----

41. I can say "no" without guilt.

_____

_____

42. I can control my own happiness.

_____

_____

43. I will live my best life.

_____

_____

44. I bring value to the world.

_____

_____

45. I am committed to having a great life.

----

46. I am in charge of my life.

----

47. I am at peace.

----

48. I will take time for me, without guilt.

----

49. I will smile today.

_____

_____

50. I am smart.

_____

51. I am a valuable member of my community.

_____

_____

52. I am talented.

_____

53. I can dream.

_____

54. I have enough.

_____

55. I am enough.

_____

56. I do enough.

_____

57. Everything I need is within me.

_____

_____

58. My life is worth living.

_____

_____

59. I am a priority in my own life.

_____

_____

60. I can be focused.

_____

61. I am determined.

_____

62. I am kind.

_____

63. I can share my feelings with others that I trust.

_____

_____

64. I am trustworthy.

_____

_____

65. My health is a priority.

_____

_____

66. I love my body.

_____

67. I am listening to my heart.

_____

_____

68. I am going to be okay.

_____

_____

69. It is okay to ask for help.

_____

_____

70. I will practice self-care daily.

_____

71. I will survive this.

_____

72. I will overcome.

_____

73. I will walk my own path.

_____

_____

74. I can do it.

_____

_____

75. This feeling is only temporary.

_____

_____

76. I believe in myself.

_____

77. I am proud of my improvements.

_____

_____

78. I am in charge of how I feel.

_____

_____

79. I am beautiful.

_____

80. I choose peace today.

_____

_____

81. I am stronger than I think.

_____

_____

82. I am thankful.

_____

83. I forgive myself.

_____

84. I forgive others for me, not for them.

_____

_____

85. I am stronger than my problems.

_____

_____

86. I know my worth.

_____

_____

87. I deserve to be treated well.

_____

_____

88. I am successful.

_____

_____

89. I am proud of my big and small victories.

_____

_____

90. My future is bright.

_____

91. I will get through this.

_____

_____

92. I will turn my dreams into goals.

_____

_____

93. I have the ability to learn new things.

_____

_____

94. I am blessed.

_____

95. I am a hard worker.

_____

_____

96. I will not speak negatively to myself or others.

_____

_____

97. I will breathe in positive energy and breath out
    negativity.

_____

_____

98. I am mighty.

_____

99. I will succeed.

_____

100.   I might stumble, but I will NEVER quit!

_____

_____

Three Generations of Cosmetologists: My mom, me, my oldest daughter. "Our legacy continues to grow."

About the Author

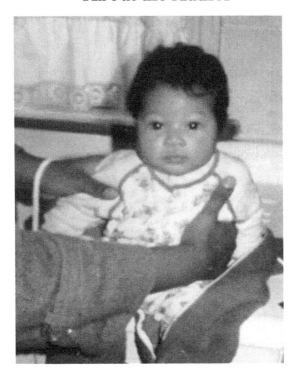

With over 20-years of experience, Atiya Johnson is known as one of South Jersey's most respected hair stylist in the game with the unique ability to craft high-quality, custom wigs in less than 45-minutes. As proud owner of Jana's Hair Salon in Lindenwold, New Jersey, Atiya specializes in natural hair care, extensions, coloring, and precision cutting. Her goal is to ensure clients leave with a memorable salon experience that exceeds their expectations. Her mission is to educate, empower and help women seeking beautiful, healthy, and natural hair.

In addition to providing exemplary hair services, Atiya's hair care line, The Seven Collection, consist of the highest quality shampoos, conditioners, and hair treatments for all hair types. When developing the line, she didn't want to compromise on any detail, therefore, each product has been tested to ensure that it delivers the best results for truly healthy hair. The Seven Collection also carries a large array of Indian, Brazilian, and Malaysian hair extensions.

To shine a spotlight on the amazing hair trends and superior hair professionals coming out of South Jersey, Atiya launched her very own Beauty & Barber Fest, which showcased some of the best hair stylist and barbers in the area. The event acted as a bridge to connect industry professionals and allowed salons the opportunity to put their creativity and technical knowledge to the test.

Motivated by the love for the beauty industry and her passion for quality education, Atiya has started the journey of creating the "first black-owned" cosmetology school in New Jersey! Throughout this journey, she has been reminded that she is a pioneer of not only the beauty industry, but strength in adversity. Just as Malcom X, Amelia Earhart, and Madam C.J. Walker were met with resistance in defying the odds against what society defined as "staying in your place"; Atiya continues to change the narrative.

With a long lineage of family in the beauty industry, Atiya took over her family beauty empire at only 17-years-old. She has a passion for helping women and being that listening ear. From behind the chair, she has coached women dealing with relationship issues, divorce and family problems helping them through their own personal trials and tribulations. To expand these gifts, Atiya decided to write her first book entitled, F.U.C.K. the Naysayers: A Kueen Making King Moves. This book takes readers on a journey into the lives of real women including Atiya who has been through challenges in life but continue to strive for greatness. She is hopeful that this book will become a useful guide for women around the world to help them push past their enemy's and naysayers to become the best version of themselves.

Atiya is happily married to Dwayne Johnson with two beautiful daughters and one son.

Atiya and Dwayne. Shown with children (l-r): Dayanna, Anisah, DJ

Stay Connected!

website: Atiyajohnson.com/Fthenaysayers